FEAST *for a* HEALTHY HEART

AROONA REEJHSINGHANI

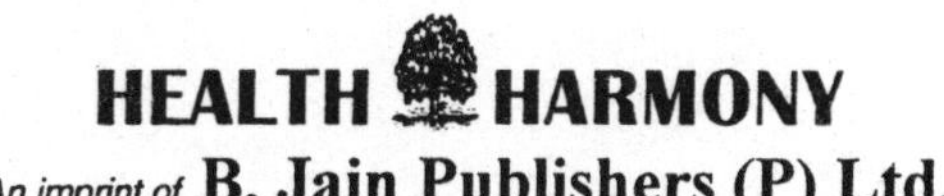

An imprint of B. Jain Publishers (P) Ltd.
An ISO 9001 : 2000 Certified Company
USA — EUROPE — INDIA

FEAST FOR A HEALTHY HEART

First Edition: 2002
Reprint Edition: 2007

Published by :
Kuldeep Jain
For

HEALTH HARMONY
an imprint of
B. Jain Publishers (P) Ltd.
1921, Street No. 10, Chuna Mandi,
Paharganj, New Delhi 110 055 (INDIA)
Phones: 91-11-2358 0800, 2358 1100, 2358 1300, 2358 3100
Fax: 91-11-2358 0471; *Email:* bjain@vsnl.com
Website: **www.bjainbooks.com**

Printed in India by
Akash Press, New Delhi-110 020

BOOK CODE / ISBN: 978-81-319-0196-0

BIODATA

Aroona Reejhsinghani

Aroona Reejhshinghani is an intellectual luminary of international repute and a human dynamo of hard work and unstinted service. Aroona belongs to the ebullient, efficient and effulgent generation and has earned rich laurels in the role of literature, social activities and social work.

She is a prolific writer and has been regularly contributing articles to various prestigious magazines, newspapers and periodicals on diverse subjects such as cookery, health, beautycare, child care, nutrition, poetries, short stories, children's stories. To her writing has been more than a career and a profession. She considers it as a "Sacred Sadhana" she has volumes of articles and writings to her credit and is authoress of 150 books. Sincere and steadfast services rendered in a spirit of dedication has brought in its wake a number of spontaneous and prestigious awards in quick succession like petals of rose.

At the age of ten won the first award for writing organized by the most prestigious magazine "Spectator", published from USA. At the age of 15 won the most outstanding dancer award from her school Mount Marys Convent, Bandra. At the age of 18 she won the best student award from her college kibhinchand Chellaram College, Bombay.

Inbetween she won a number of prizes as a kathak dancer. She was dramatic, and then general secretary of her college and also founder of students association of her college.

Her first book *Womans World* came out when she was eighteen and since them she has not looked back. She is consulting editor of many prestigious poetry magazines, published from Mangalore and Uttar Pradesh. She is on the governing council and on the editorial board of "International Socio-literary Foundation". She was editor in chief of Cuisine, India's first and most prestigious magazine on food for some time. She was founder editor of her own magazine "Aroona's world of food", which she ran successfully for some years. She was a columnist for hindi magazine "Manorama", "Free Press Journal", "Navbharat Times and Deccan Herald". In 1991 she entered the Limca Book of Records. Guiness Book of World Records has also congratulated her on her unique achievements. Her biography was included in 1976 in the directory of Great Indian women, where all the leading great women of those days were listed. She entered American Book of Honour in 1980. She was nominated for the prestigious title of being the most outstanding personality of the last 100 years by the American Biographical Institute in 1999. Her name was included in the book "International Directory of Distinguished Leadership", USA. She was awarded the AFGA National Award for excellence in appreciation for her contribution in the field of freelance journalism in 1993. She was declared as an International Personality of 2001 by International Biographical Institute, Cambridge, England. She was honored with Winged Word Award in 2001 by International Socio-literary Foundation, Chennai. She was nominated as being amongst 2000 Outstanding of the 21st Century by IBC, England. She was also given the "21st Century Award for Achievement" in recognition for her outstanding contribution to literature. She was nominated as the "International Women of the Year", in 2001 by Cambridge, England. Today she is featured in numerous sites on the internet. Her name has been included in all the prestigious sites in the world from USA to Canada from Kandhar to Pakistan, from Japan to China. She has been featured with most of the leading lights of the last and this century, no matter whether they were freedom fighters, great literary giants or even prime ministers.

PREFACE

The human heart is the sturdiest and toughest organ of the body. It is designed to last you a lifetime. But because of wrong eating habits at a young age this most important organ of our body refuses to work properly. This is my second book on heart diseases, the first book became a leading best seller. This book too I hope will enjoy as much popularity as my first book. This book contains a sensible selection of low-fat and low-cholesterol foods. These foods provide ammunition against cholesterol accumulation and lower the cholesterol levels thus preventing heart disease and thus helping in keeping this most important organ healthy and strong. Besides teaching you how to prepare a sensible diet, this book also answers all the questions you ever wanted to know about the working of heart, about high cholesterol and blood pressure. This book is a must, not only for heart patients but for everyone who wants to live with a healthy heart.

Aroona Reejhsinghani

CONTENTS

Chapter 1

INTRODUCTION

The Heart

Heart is one of the most important organs in the human body. If the heart beats, your life beats, if your heart stops then your life stops its journey on this earth.

It is situated in the center of the chest a little to the left then to the right. It is responsible for pumping blood into your system and keeping you alive. In a state of repose the heart pumps five liters of blood in a minute. Its output goes up to fifteen to twenty or even thirty liters per minute when you are engaged in some strenuous exercise. It pumps about 182 million liters of blood. It does this by means of the most intricately woven muscle in the body. The blood travels to all parts of the body and returns to the heart after being purified in the lungs in fifteen seconds.

The heart beats in an adult 72 times a minute, in times of stress the beat may reach double its normal reading with the blood pressure going up accordingly. If the arteries become diseased with fatty deposits clogging them then the heart has to exert more pressure to send the blood through the arteries, when this happens a condition known as hypertension or high blood pressure is born. If this condition is left untreated it may lead to heart disease.

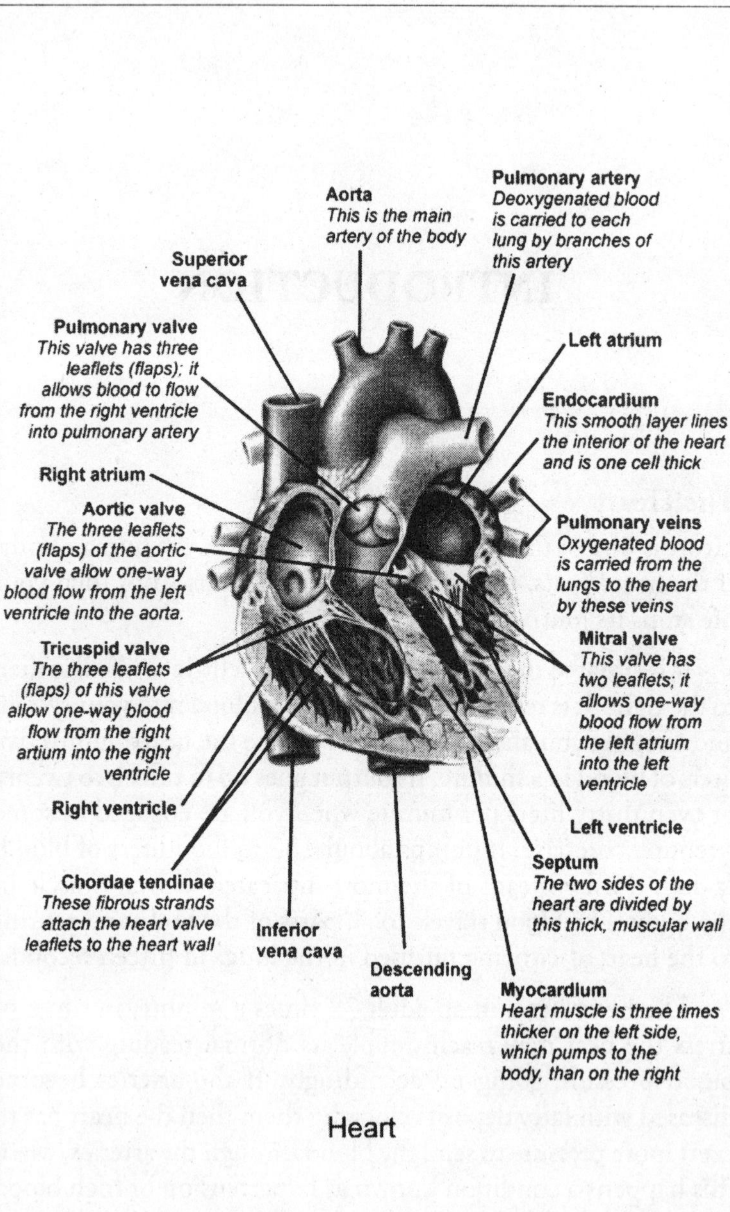
Aorta
This is the main artery of the body
Pulmonary artery
Deoxygenated blood is carried to each lung by branches of this artery
Superior vena cava
Pulmonary valve
This valve has three leaflets (flaps); it allows blood to flow from the right ventricle into pulmonary artery
Left atrium
Endocardium
This smooth layer lines the interior of the heart and is one cell thick
Right atrium
Aortic valve
The three leaflets (flaps) of the aortic valve allow one-way blood flow from the left ventricle into the aorta.
Pulmonary veins
Oxygenated blood is carried from the lungs to the heart by these veins
Tricuspid valve
The three leaflets (flaps) of this valve allow one-way blood flow from the right artium into the right ventricle
Mitral valve
This valve has two leaflets; it allows one-way blood flow from the left atrium into the left ventricle
Right ventricle
Left ventricle
Septum
The two sides of the heart are divided by this thick, muscular wall
Chordae tendinae
These fibrous strands attach the heart valve leaflets to the heart wall
Inferior vena cava
Descending aorta
Myocardium
Heart muscle is three times thicker on the left side, which pumps to the body, than on the right

Heart

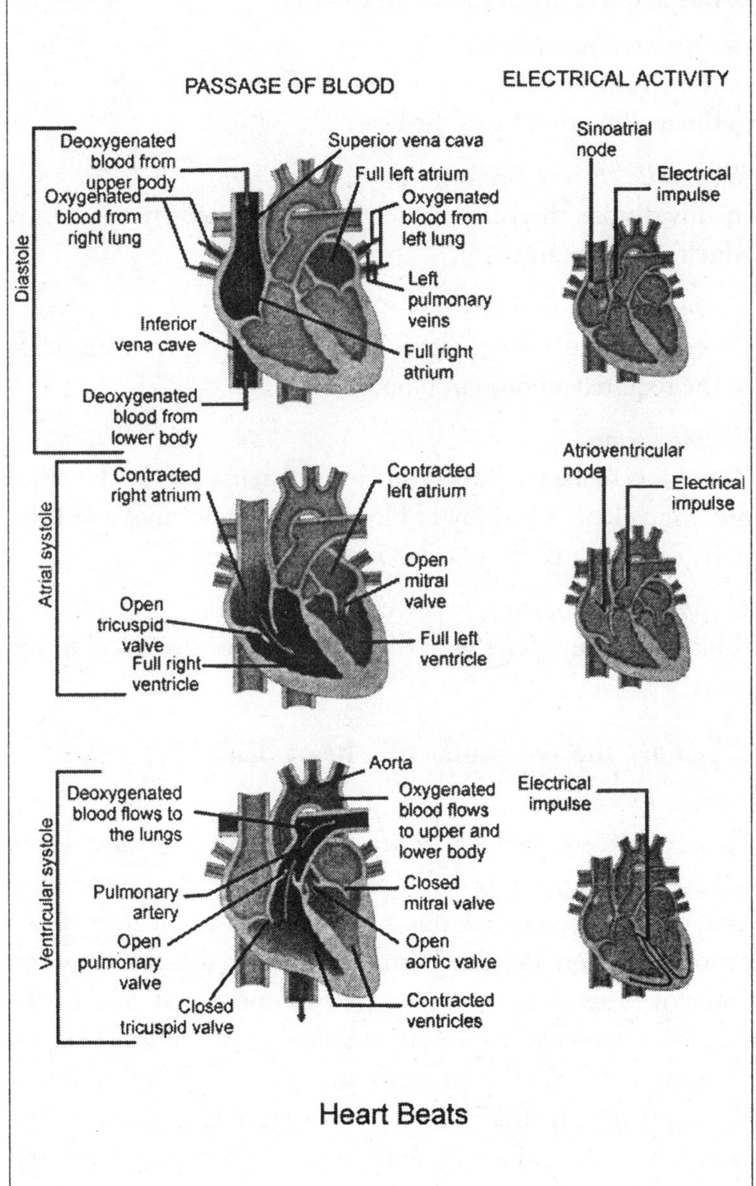
PASSAGE OF BLOOD
ELECTRICAL ACTIVITY
Diastole
Deoxygenated blood from upper body
Oxygenated blood from right lung
Superior vena cava
Full left atrium
Oxygenated blood from left lung
Left pulmonary veins
Inferior vena cave
Full right atrium
Deoxygenated blood from lower body
Sinoatrial node
Electrical impulse
Atrial systole
Contracted right atrium
Contracted left atrium
Open mitral valve
Open tricuspid valve
Full right ventricle
Full left ventricle
Atrioventricular node
Electrical impulse
Ventricular systole
Aorta
Deoxygenated blood flows to the lungs
Oxygenated blood flows to upper and lower body
Pulmonary artery
Closed mitral valve
Open pulmonary valve
Open aortic valve
Closed tricuspid valve
Contracted ventricles
Electrical impulse

Heart Beats

What are the ailments of the heart?

Congenital Heart Disease.

In this disease a baby is born with a defective valve which leads to the malfunctioning of the heart.

Rheumatic Heart Disease.

In this disease the heart muscles are weakened by the germs which cause rheumatism.

Coronary Heart Disease.

Defective circulation of blood in the arteries deprives the heart of the required amount of blood.

Angine Pectoris.

There is a violent paroxysm of painful sensation in the chest due to inadequate supply of blood to the inner muscles of the heart or myocardium as called in medical terms.

Coronary Thrombosis

A blood clot interferes with the circulation of the blood to the heart.

What are the symptoms of a heart disease?

Pain in the chest.

Heart pain associated with a heart attack is very specific. There is a powerful squeezing feeling and a great weight on the chest as though someone has put a grinding stone on it. A sharp shooting pain on the other hand very often is a sign of indigestion and not heart disease; it is caused by too much acid in the stomach or it may be due to the disease of the gall bladder. Sometimes the sharp pain may indicate a disorder called mitral valve prolapse. It effects about 20 percent of elder women. The condition occurs as mitral valve in the heart opens and closes. Normally the valve should close tightly to prevent blood from leaking backwards into the upper chamber of the heart. Prolapse occurs when the valve fails to close tightly and some blood flows backwards. This can cause chest pain and other symptoms including shortness of breath, dizziness and fatigue. Although its not a serious condition it should be referred to a doctor.

Suffocation.
The second indication is suffocation. The patient finds it very difficult to breathe, sometimes due to this the face turns blue.

Pain in the Left Arm and Behind the Left Shoulder.
One of the other symptoms of heart attack is pain traveling down the left shoulder and arm; if you experience this type of pain you may start fearing the worst, but the key is if the pain radiating out from the chest is not associated with chest pain, the chances are that the pain in your arm is caused by bursitis, arthritis or simple muscle strain.

Irregular Pulse.
An healthy adult has a pulse of 72 times a minute. If the pause between one pulse beat and the next is irregular it means that the heart is not doing its job properly.

Nausea and Vomiting.
If you suffer from frequent attacks of nausea and vomiting and you are a patient of high blood pressure it indicates defect in the working of your heart and arteries.

Sweating.
If profuse sweating is accompanied by a feeling of coldness in the body then see your doctor immediately.

Irregular Respiration.
If the heart does not function properly the blood supply to the lungs is interrupted and the breathing becomes irregular. You may draw one long breath and then a short one or the pause between one breath and the second one may be long. This is

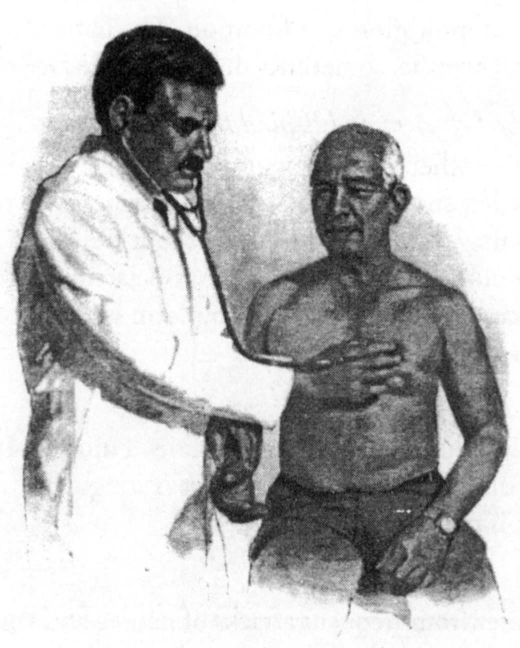

Physical Examination

one of the leading symptoms of heart disease which should not be ignored.

Dryness of the Mouth.
Dryness of the mouth is due to many reasons, but if with the dryness of the mouth you have difficulty in swallowing and have one or more of the symptoms described above then see your physician.

Pain in the Joints.
Pain in the joints should not be ignored because they may be due to rheumatic heart disease. It is a disease of adolescence which rarely attacks adults.

Chronic Indigestion.
Sometimes indigestion is due to malfunctioning of the heart so if it persists ask your physician to check you thoroughly.

Flushed Face.
If the flushing occurs in combination with palpitation then you may have a heart problem, if not this could be due to disorder of the adrenal or thyroid gland or kidney.

Cold Hands and Feet.
This is common amongst older people. Usually cold hands and feet are the result of poor circulation and not heart disease. You may have arteriosclerosis (diminished blood flow due to plaque buildup) in the large blood vessels in your legs or a vascular inflammation (spasms of the small arteries in the hands or feet causing them to turn red and feel numb). Sometimes poor circulation maybe the result of diabetes.

Light Headedness.
Feeling light headed and weak when getting up from a chair or after bending down to pick something is related to your blood pressure or anemia, so see your doctor.

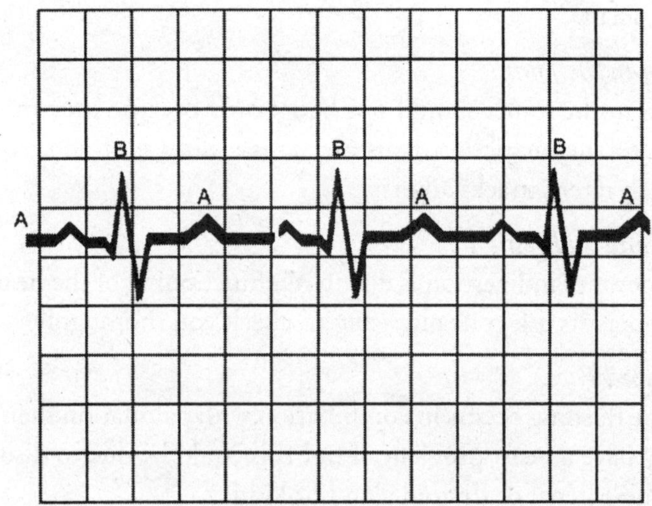

Electrocardiogram

Electrical current generated by the heart is picked up by small metal contacts placed against the skin. These messages are then transmitted to a sensitive recording mechanism called an electrocardiograph.

I hear that depression too is one of the greatest causes of heart attacks?

Severe depression is also a big risk factor in developing coronary artery disease (CAD). Early diagnosis and treatment of depression is very essential to save a life.

What are the other factors which give rise to attacks?

Other major factors are cigarette smoking, high cholesterol levels and high blood pressure.

Palpitation

Palpitation is forceful beating of the heart which makes a person aware of the heartbeats. Occasional palpitations maybe due to anxiety, stress or due to too much consumption of coffee or tea, however if it occurs often especially if you are above the age of 35 and suffering from high blood pressure you must immediately see a doctor.

How do you treat palpitation?

Palpitation is very frightening, some palpitations are dangerous but most are not. It may be helpful to avoid smoking, coffee, tea, alcohol and some cold medicines. Persistent palpitation may require drug therapy. Such drugs are known as anti-arhythmic drugs and are to be taken under the supervision of a doctor.

What is ECG test?

An ECG (electrocardiogram) is one of the most common tests done to diagnose heart ailments. But ECG does not always give a correct picture of the condition of the heart therefore doctors rely on stress test. Stress test is more reliable then ECG.

How is stress test done?

The test consists of a plank with a moving belt on which the patient is made to walk and ECG, pulse rate and blood pressure

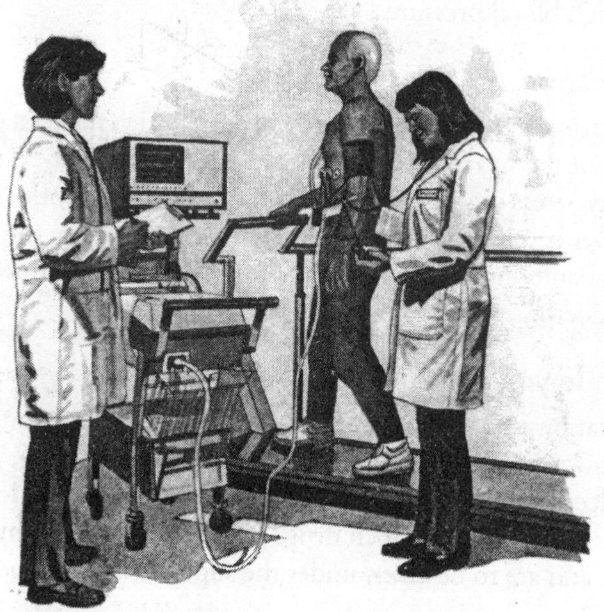

A Treadmill test

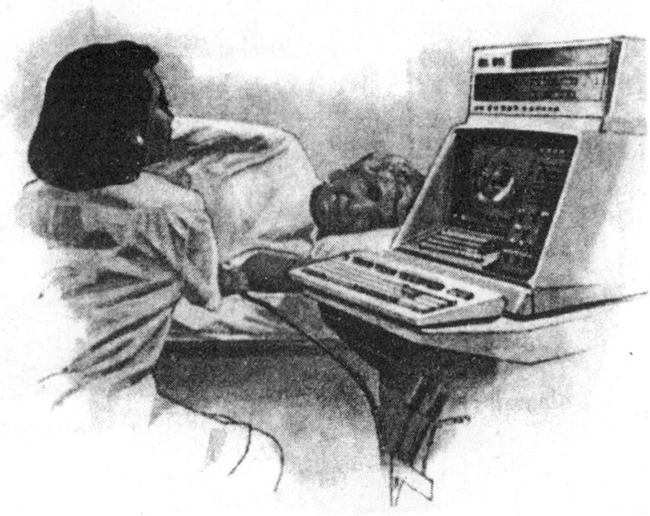

Echocardiography

An echocardiogram shows the structure and movement of your heart muscle. While you rest, sound waves bounce off your heart and are converted into a picture on a screen. The test shows whether your heart is enlarged, the thickness of the heart's walls, whether there are problems with the heart's valves, and how well the heart pumps.

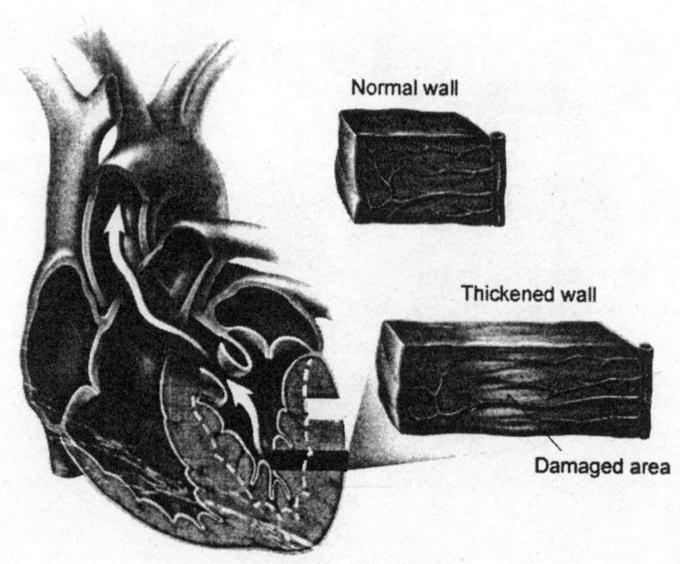

Hypertensive Heart Disease

are monitored by a computer. The patient is made to walk at different speeds for 6 minutes till a particular heart rate is achieved.

Who needs a stress test?

Any person with chest pain and symptoms of breathlessness suspected to be due to coronary heart disease.

Who should avoid stress test?

1. A person suffering from anginal chest pains.
2. A person suffering from irregular heartbeats or more than 12 irregular beats per minute.
3. Anybody suffering from breathlessness and cough which becomes severe when lying down and gets relief when he is upright.
4. A person having uncontrolled high blood pressure.
5. If there is any infection in any part of the body.

If blood pressure is the main cause of heart disease, how do I control it or avoid it?

Exercise regularly for atleast half an hour daily. Stop smoking, smoking and alcohol raises the blood pressure. Potassium reduces blood pressure, potatoes are rich in potassium. Eat baked potatoes with a sprinkling of salt daily. Eat only steamed or baked vegetables, boiling vegetables robs them of a good amount of potassium and magnesium. Sacrifice sodium; many people with high blood pressure are effected by sodium in the salt. Sodium sensitive people retain more fluid which in turn raises the BP. Try to reduce your salt intake as much as you can. Declare war on pickles, papads, salted biscuits, canned foods, burgers, pizzas, Chinese foods which contain ajinomotto. Calcium helps you to

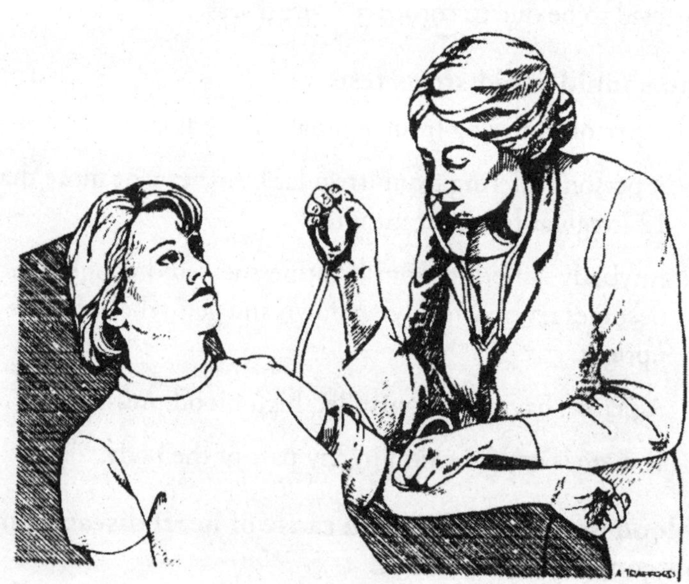

Blood Pressure

There are two distinct aspects of every heartbeat -the peak of the heartbeat, or contractions (called the systole), and the pause between beats, or relaxation (called the diastole). As a consequence, there are two aspects to any blood pressure reading. Your physician will record a two-number reading (i.e. 120/80, to be read, one-twenty over eighty), the first number being the systolic reading, and the second, the diastolic reading.

put a good fight against hypertension and milk is rich in calcium. A glass of milk a day keeps hypertension at bay. Milk contains tryptophan which besides being a natural tranquilizer also triggers off serotonin, a chemical messenger in the brain believed responsible for lowering the blood pressure. Besides, learn to relax at all times, do not lose your cool always. Enjoy yourself, go for walks, make friends and in short take it easy.

What should be my normal pressure?

A blood pressure reading of 140/90 is generally considered high however most doctors now regard upper reading of 100 plus the age of the patient as acceptable pressure and not high blood pressure.

Does diet reduces pressure?

Diet certainly reduces pressure. Eat a diet made up of fruits, vegetables, milk, curds and cereals like makai, jower, rajmah, bajra. Onion, garlic and strawberries lower the pressure. Replace tea, coffee and cold drinks with herb teas or juices of celery grapefruits, oranges, cucumber and pineapple. Fish is also helpful in reducing pressure. Fish like tuna, bangla, mackerel and surmai should be eaten atleast thrice a week. Also beans should be included in your daily diet. They give you as much proteins as meat and also lower the blood cholesterol. They are low in sodium and high in potassium; they are not only good for patients of high blood pressure but also for heart patients. Vitamin E supplements are also said to lower blood pressure considerably; potatoes and bananas also lower blood pressure, two bananas a day keeps blood pressure at bay.

Vitamins and heart

Vitamin A

Vitamin a reduces blood cholesterol if given along with vitamin D.

Given in conjunction with vitamin E it prevents deposition of fat in the arteries.

Vitamin B (thiamin)

Thiamin deficiency impairs the functioning of the heart; increases the tendency of extravascular fluid collections and results in terminal cardiac standstill. Its deficiency is also the cause of degeneration of the muscles of the heart.

Lack of it also causes Beri Beri or enlargement of the heart, excessive alcohol has also similar effects on the heart.

Vitamin C

Vitamin C lowers the cholesterol in the blood. It has been found that the highest sufferers of cholesterol in the blood are those whose diet is lacking in this vital vitamin.

Vitamin D

Vitamin D together with vitamin A keeps the cholesterol in the blood to manageable limit. The second and the biggest advantage of this vitamin is to help the body absorb calcium, lack of which can produce coronary distress. Calcium also helps the heart to beat with regularity.

Vitamin E

Vitamin E retards the clotting of blood. If there is any clot produced in the blood it helps the arteries to pass it through without causing their blockage. Some doctors even believe that a regular use of this vitamin can even prevent a heart attack. This vital vitamin is available in sprouts and certain vegetable oils, therefore try to eat more of sprouted foods.

Minerals and heart

Calcium

It plays a vital role in the beating of the heart. If there is a lack of this mineral in the body the muscles of the heart will not contract properly and the blood will get clotted. The result will also be a weakening of the heartbeats. Calcium cannot work alone, it has to be helped by magnesium in the system for the heart to contract and relax. It is magnesium which helps the muscles of the heart to contract and relax; not only the muscles of the body but even other organs of the body are helped by magnesium. Magnesium also avoids high blood pressure. Every movement, external or internal, is triggered by impulses transmitted along the nerves and it is magnesium which controls these impulses.

Potassium

Potassium is another mineral, lack of which can create complications of the heart. It is sometimes substituted for sodium chloride (Common salt) for patients of heart diseases. If potassium is lacking in the body the muscles of the heart start degenerating leading to heart failure. A proper combination of potassium and magnesium helps the heart to withstand stress, this is because of the ability of potassium to maintain power of the heart muscles.

Chromium

Chromium plays a big role in keeping the cholesterol levels down. It also has a role in the metabolism of carbohydrates.

Zinc

Low zinc levels can cause hardening of arteries which may prove fatal. In some cases of hardening of arteries when zinc was given in 200 mg doses thrice daily, the patient showed remarkable recovery.

Phosphorus

Phosphorus helps in the assimilation of calcium into the system. It also helps the metabolism of fats and carbohydrates.

Iron

Iron is essential for the formation of the red blood corpulales in the body. Lack of iron can lead to anemia and this disorder can lead to many serious heart ailments.

From the above article you can deduce that the diet of the heart patients should be well-balanced which contains all the vitamins and minerals to lead a healthy and a happy life.

What is cholesterol?

Cholestrol is a waxy material which helps in many of the body's chemical processes. If it is in correct amount in the body it provides us with good health but too much of it in the blood encourages the development of arteriosclerosis and this gives rise to coronary heart disease.

Foods that increase cholesterol are saturated fats. These are mostly found in animal foods such as beef, lamb, ham, butter, cream, whole milk, cheese, ghee, coconut oil and palm oil. The oils that lower the blood cholesterol are cotton sead oil, sunflower oil, till oil and corn oil. These oils are called polyunsaturated oils. The other foods containing high cholesterol are organ meats such as liver, kidney, heart and brain; shell fish such as oysters, crabs, prawns, shrimps, scallops, lobsters, egg yolks, chicken fat, lard, bacon, red meat, cream, rich sauces, gravies, pastries, mayonnaise sauce and fried foods such as wafers, patties, samosas, etc. Other foods which are to be avoided are cakes, pastries, pudding, egg noodles, etc. because all these things contain eggs.

What are the foods which lower cholesterol?

You can eat egg white because it is high in proteins and contains no cholesterol. You can eat fish especially white fish like pomfret, halibut and white salmon and chicken without the skin. Beans and lentils can be used instead of meat since they are a storehouse of proteins. Apples, papayas and lichis are good cholesterol reducers especially apples which are very useful in lowering cholesterol. Garlic is also a cholesterol reducer; it also reduces blood pressure. Another important food item which lowers blood cholesterol is alfa and carrots.

Is sugar harmful for the heart?

According to research a person who takes more sugar has more risk of being a heart patient. Besides plain sugar, carbohydrates and starch also should be avoided because they transform into glucose in the body. Instead of sugar you can take honey. It can any day replace white sugar which is called white poison. Dr. John Yudkin a leading English nutritionist has come out with the theory that sugar is the main heart attack villain. He says that it is sugar that for reasons yet unknown leads the body to manufacture a type of cholesterol that forms deposits inside the blood vessels and clogs them. White sugar being devoid of vitamins and minerals is aptly described as "nutritional death trap". Honey is a wonderful substitute for sugar. The secret of honey's virtue lies in its principal ingredient called "Sugar Dextrose." Dextrose is oxidized by all the tissues of the body to provide energy; ordinarily more then half the body's energy is provided by the burning of dextrose. Muscles and other tissues remove dextrose from the blood to form glycogen which yields energy for tissue machinery. Dextrose is the only form in which sugar can be stored in the body and it is therefore readily available for use when energy is required by the body. Honey is a golden wonder, full of nutritional properties which can be used safely by everyone.

Besides sugar you should also avoid spices and chilies. A little salt and pepper added to food may not look so alluring but it is safer in the long run.

Is coffee and alcohol bad for the heart?

Coffee has a tendency to create vitamin deficiency in the body; such deficiencies can cause serious disorders in the body that may make it difficult for your heart to function properly. Sometimes it is given to heart patients because it expands the arteries and furnishes a better blood supply, but if taken in too much quantity it may prove harmful if the heart is diseased.

Smoking should be stopped alltogether if you are a heart patient because experiments have shown that heart rate increase by five per minute after you have smoked one cigarette. Nicotine in tobacco not only destroys vitamin C in the body but also it increases fat levels in the blood making the patient a victim of coronary failure. Normally a heart patient should not imbibe liquor but if taken in moderation it can prove helpful because it quickens the circulation of blood and reduces pressure on the heart.

What type of exercise should a heart patient undertake to keep fit and healthy?

The best exercise for a heart patient is walking. You can start with 15 minutes of daily walking then you can go on increasing the time limit; if you can walk for an hour without feeling the strain then you are on the way to becoming healthy again.

Should a heart patient give up sex?

Heart patients can indulge in sex after asking their doctors for specific instructions before indulging in the act. But here are some guidelines.

Never engage in sexual activity when you have a full stomach; never engage in it when it is extreme hot or extremely cold season.

Do not have sex when you have had alcohol. Do not engage in sex when you are tired, take rest before going in for it.

Here are a few warning signs when you indulge in sexual activity: If the chest pain occurs during the activity and continues afterwards, it is a sure sign that your heart has been taxed; if the pulse rate does not return to normal within 15 minutes and the shortness of breath continues beyond 15 minutes, its time to see a doctor.

What is X syndrome and how does it increases the risk of heart attack?

X syndrome is a cluster of symptoms which increases the risk of heart attacks. Some of the symptoms are high cholesterol, high blood pressure, high fasting blood sugar that is type two diabetes, fat mainly around the abdomen, chronic fatigue and difficulty in losing weight. You can either increase or decrease your risk of having X syndrome by eating a right diet. First step towards eating a right diet: take a personal interest in developing and maintaining good health. Educate yourself on the health risks that are associated with bad eating habits. Replace fats, starches and sugars with fruits and nuts. Snack on popcorn or rabbit foods like cucumber and carrot sticks instead of fried samosas, patties, kababs and fingerchips. Use mustard instead of mayonnaise sauce in your sandwiches. Replace airated water with fruits and vegetable juices. Red meat should be avoided, instead eat lean fish and young chicken without the skin. Go in for brown bread instead of white, instead of ice cream and creamy desserts use skimmed milk curds sweetened with honey and decorated with fresh fruits. Discard sugar and use honey and jaggery as sweeteners. Avoid fast and fried foods like pizzas, burgers, parathas, puries.

Exercise daily; even mild physical exercise helps a lot. Half an hour a day of physical activity is all that it takes to keep yourself in good health. Choose the stairs instead of the elevator.

Measuring Blood Pressure

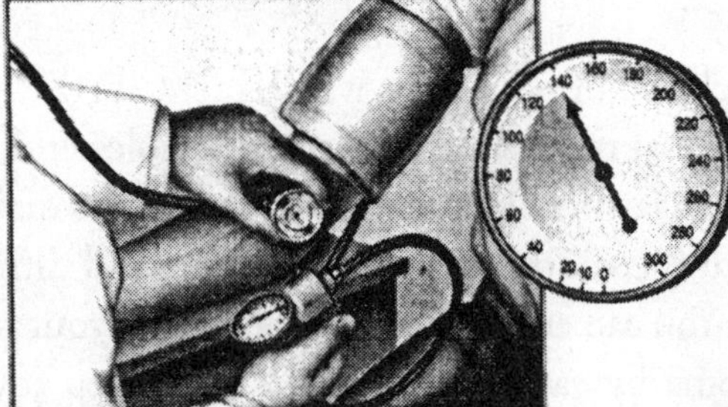

Normal below

140 mm Hg Systolic
90 mm Hg Diastolic

High Blood Pressure, i.e.,

180 mm Hg Systolic
105 mm Hg Diastolic

The Effects of Hypertension on the Heart

Hypertension, or high blood pressure, causes the heart to work harder to circulate blood. This added workload results in a thickened muscle wall that demands more blood supply. During strenuous activities, such as exercise, blood supply levels may not be sufficient to meet this new demand and can result in damage to the muscle wall. This progressive damage can ultimately lead to congestive heart failure where the heart muscle is unable to pump blood properly.

Taking the stairs is like taking your heart for a healthy walk. Besides just taking walk for half an hour 3 times a week helps to slow down the loss of minerals from your bones, improves fitness, cardiovascular health, strengthens bones and muscles and facilitates better weight management. Even slow walking keeps your body in a fit condition. The solution to the control of X syndrome lies with you; eat sensibly and exercise regularly and you will never fall a victim to a heart disease.

Can fish protect you from heart disease?

Recent studies have shown that if you eat fish at least once every week you have a lower risk of sudden cardiac arrest. Fish contains a specific type of saturated fat made up of omega-3 fatty acids that appear to be good for human beings. Fish high on omega-3 fat include salmon, mackerel, tuna and sardines. Eating fish instead of red meat you automatically choose a dish lower in saturated fat better for blood cholesterol levels and possibly protection against cancer.

I hear that if you drink tea you are insured against heart problems?

A study conducted at the American College of Cardiology suggests that drinking black tea may be good for your heart. It was noted that tea which is rich in antioxidants called flavnoids might protect the cells and tissues against oxidative damage associated with cardiovascular disease. Another study suggest that the incidence of heart diseases decreased by 11 percent by drinking 3 cups of black tea per day; it also supports cardiovascular health; it prevents clotting and increases antioxidants concentrated in the blood.

Can you suggest how one can survive a heart attack till the appearance of medical help?

If you suddenly start experiencing a severe pain in the chest which radiates into your arm and into your jaw and you start feeling faint then immediately take an aspirin if you are at home but if you are not at home then forget the aspirin and start coughing vigorously and repeatedly. A deep breath should be taken before each cough and the cough must be deep and prolonged like when coughing out sputum from deep inside the chest. A breath and a cough must be repeated about every two seconds without letup till the heart breathes normally again.

Deep breathing gets oxygen into the lungs and coughing movements squeeze the heart and keep the blood circulating. The squeeze pressure on the heart also helps to regain normal rhythm. In this way you can have higher chances of surviving a heart attack, but even if you feel normal, rush yourself to a hospital in case of heart attack.

What is the meaning of "systolic and diastolic" blood pressure?

Hypertension increase the risk of having a heart disease, stroke or kidney failure. It is recommended that you have a blood pressure reading every two years. A blood pressure reading is really two measurements in one, with one written over the other such as 120/80. The upper number is known as systolic pressure which represents the amount of pressure in the blood vessels when the heart contracts (beats) and pushes blood through the circulatory system. The lower number is known as diastolic pressure which represents the pressure in the blood vessels between beats when the heart is resting. Normal blood pressure is below 130/85 and high normal is between 130/85 and 139/89.

I hear that beans and peas in our regular diet can lower the risk of heart disease?

According to a recent study people eating beans and peas at least 4 times a week had 22 percent lower risk of coronary heart disease than those who consumed them once a week. The more you eat these beans the less likely you will get high blood pressure, high cholesterol and diabetes. They are rich in soluble fiber which has been seen to lower high cholesterol and improve insulin resistance. They contain low levels of sodium, high levels of potassium, calcium and magnesium – a combination which is associated with a reduced risk of heart disease.

What is blood pressure?

Blood pressure is the force of your heart pumping blood to all the organs in your body. The pressure measured when the heart is contracting is called systolic pressure. The diastolic pressure is measured when the heart is at rest. These two values make up the blood pressure.

Can I measure my own blood pressure accurately?

Yes you can. There are blood pressure monitoring machines now available in the market. Do not exert yourself for at least half an hour before taking your blood pressure. Sit down and rest your left arm on the table, palm up and at heart level. Place the cuff around the upper arm or wrist depending upon the type of instrument you are using. Adjust the cuff on the blood pressure meter so that it is not too tight or loose. Start measuring the blood pressure. Do not talk or move about unnecessarily. Wait atleast 10 minutes between each measurement. Measure your blood pressure at the same time every day.

A friend a day and keeping a pet I hear keeps the doctor away?

According to a recent study carried out by doctors at Harvard School of Public Health at Boston, people who have a large number of friends, relatives, other social ties live longer and healthier lives, then people who live isolated lives. Psychotherapists are becoming increasingly aware of value of

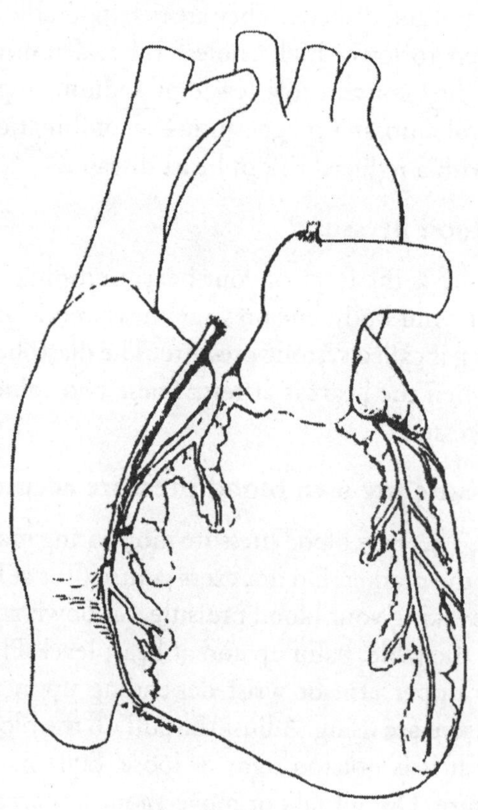

Bypass

When atherosclerosis has narrowed or obstructed segments of the coronary arteries, a bypass operation is performed to connect clear passages above and below the blockage. An arterial graft is constructed using a vein or artery taken from another (non-essential) part of the body or from tubing made of Dacron. The natural healing process secures the graft and effects a life-saving 'detour'. Adequate blood flow to the heart is restored as the blood re-routes around the narrow or occluded portions of existing vessels.

pets in treating emotional, physical and mental health. Pets are of particular help to the aged, the physically sick, the mentally ill and for those who suffer from a sense of rejection. Pets can restore a feeling of identify and self-worth. A pet can occasionally represent the difference between life and death. The pet is a golden chain leading to good mental and physical health.

What is angioplasty?

When the coronary artery supplying blood to the heart gets narrowed due to high fat and cholesterol deposits and fibrous tissues on the inner lining, they then obstruct the flow of blood to the heart which leads to a heart attack. Till 1976 this condition was treated with bypass surgery, but now this is treated with introduction of a balloon percutaneously in coronary arteries and busting the block. This method is more popular than bypass surgery and is called coronary angioplasty.

What is the difference between angioplasty and bypass surgery?

In angioplasty the balloon is introduced into the coronary artery from a puncture done in the groin in a fully conscious person under x-ray control. This procedure takes about an hour or so. Soon after the operation the patient is offered a light breakfast and within 24 hours he is discharged from the hospital. But bypass needs 4 hours of anesthesia, a large surgical incision on the chest, 10 days of hospitalization and 4 weeks of rest and this procedure is costlier then angioplasty.

Are there any limitations of coronary angioplasty?

Yes, there could be recurrence of the blockage at the same site in approximately thirty percent of the cases, but the recurrence rate has been brought down with drug coated stunts from 15 to 9 percent.

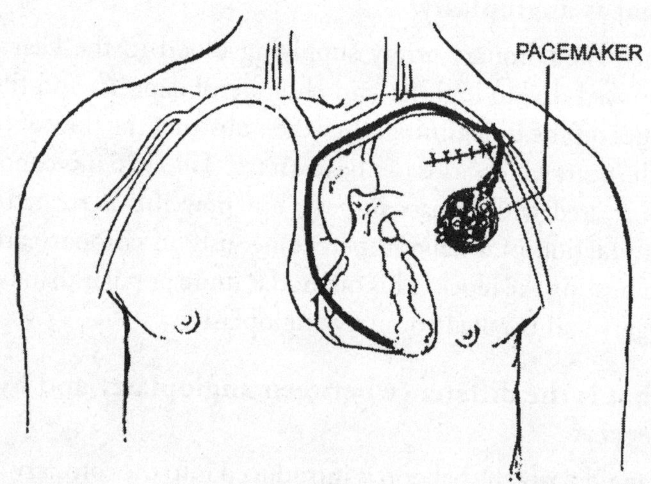

Pacemaker

Several kinds of heart disease can cause an abnormally slow heart rate. When the heart no longer functions adequately to maintain a steady rate, an artificial pacemaker is implanted to take over the task. A small, battery-powered mechanism, called a pacemaker is usually implanted under the skin and wired to the heart to control its rate and rhythm of contraction. The length of time between battery replacements varies according to the type of pacemaker and its battery supply.

We hear that cellphones could spell trouble for patients who are implanted with pacemakers?

One of the major health hazards facing cellphone users who have pacemaker implants is that the electromagnetic interference could affect the pacemaker either by stopping the pacemaker from delivering stimulating pulses that regulate the heart's rhythm, by causing the pacemaker to deliver irregular pulses or by causing the pacemaker to ignore the heart's own rhyme and deliver pulses at a fixed rate; this was found out by Food and Drug Administration of USA. Therefore, the phones are not safe for heart patients having pacemaker implants.

DIET FOR A HEALTHY HEART

Eating your way to healthy heart

No one wants to grow old, everyone wants to be young always. Is it possible to die as young as possible and as late as possible. It is not some futuristic dream but a present possibility. Research shows that a number of diseases can be prevented by eating a well balanced diet. It has been shown by scientists that children with low birth weight suffer diseases like diabetes, heart diseases, blood pressure and osteoporosis in their adult life. The birth weight can be improved with a proper diet if a mother eats a nutritious diet during pregnancy. Lack of right diet also causes energy deficiency and the inability to carry out our daily work. When there is lack of pulses, green vegetables, fresh fruits you suffer from micro-nutrient deficiency. The consequence is anemia which is serious in the women of reproductive age, adolescents and children. The most important thing is to eat green leafy vegetables like spinach and gourds. These are not only cheap but supply a whole range of vitamins, folic acid, iron and calcium. But most of the urban house wives are depending too much on carbohydrates and fats, therefore abdominal problems and chronic diseases are becoming common. So, we should always opt for a well-balanced diet which supplies all the essential nutrients to the body. It has been found that a diet which contains grains, vegetables, dals and beans and fruits provide adequate amount of all the essential nutrients. Amongst all the foods, grains are the most important and most potent of all the foods. They contain all the important nutrients needed for human growth. Grains include rice, wheat, corn, barley, oats, jowar, bajra, etc. Grains that are ground in stone ground mills are healthier and safer to eat. The extra heat provided by metal grinders destroy the enzymes, vitamin E and gluten in the grain – the essential amino acids that builds the protein value of a meal. The same happens with the dals and beans if they are not stone grounded. Bran which is the outer layer of the grain should never be discarded because it not only provides essential minerals to the body, but it also contains fiber. Fiber gives bulk to our diet which helps in pushing waste products out of our body and also absorbs toxins from the body. Eating sufficient fiber prevents constipation and helps reduce the risk of colon cancer. Fiber also makes us chew food longer and fills the stomach sooner making meals more satisfying thus preventing us from over-eating and gaining unnecessary weight. Along with grains the next important foods are dals and beans. These are rich sources of proteins and excellent sources of iron and most of the B vitamins, therefore they are called "Body builders". Vegetables and fruits come next and these are extremely rich sources of minerals, enzymes and vitamins. The greener and fresher the products, the higher are their vitamin content. Vegetables and fruit which are force ripened or exposed to heat and air and stored for long time in the fridge lose their vitamin C content. Even when they are canned, pickled or frozen they lose most of their nutrients. To prevent loss of nutrients you should try to cook vegetables with their peels (wherever possible) because the largest amount of minerals are directly under the skin and these are lost when the vegetables are peeled. Do not peel and cut in advance, always cut them when you need to cook them. Never keep fruits chopped and exposed to light because then they will lose their B vitamins. Yellow or orange coloured fruits and vegetables contain beta-carotene which is very good for maintaining healthy eyes, skin and heart. For maintenance of good health you should eat atleast 250 grams of fruits in season. About 40 percent of your food should be eaten in raw form. Every process in the body depends upon digestion and assimilation without which you cannot survive. And our body cannot go on with this process without the help of enzymes. But enzymes are only found in raw foods because heat destroys enzymes. Enzymes are produced by the body when we are young but as we age body cannot cope up with the enzyme requirements of the body, therefore to keep diseases away we should eat 40 percent of food raw either in the form of vegetables or fruits. We should start our meal with raw foods, this will prevent us from eating more and will help us not to increase in weight.

Some important hints to follow in healthy eating

Along with right eating cooking utensils are considered part of the whole system of good health. Iron utensils contain natural minerals which combat anemia. The zinc-lined brass vessels (Pital) are healthy use because they too contain essential minerals for maintain health, storing water in copper containers prevents allergies and arthiritis. Cooking in aluminum vessels reduces calcium in the body and gives rise to osteoporosis and weakness of bones. Eggs are considered rich source of proteins and minerals but since yolks are high in cholesterol they should be avoided by heart patients and they should eat only whites of eggs. Wholesome eggs come from fowls which are allowed to roam freely and find their worms by scratching manure which is usually laden with vitamins B 12, K and proteins. Desi eggs though smaller then their English counterparts are safer and richer in proteins and other nutrients.

Fish rates high in nutritional value supplying proteins which are more easily digestible than the proteins of mutton. Bangla, tarla and other oily fish contain omega-3 fatty acids that help clear the body of cholesterol.

Chicken and mutton are also rich sources of proteins which are easily digestible than the ones found in beans and dals. Birds and animals who are allowed to find their own natural fodder are wholesome and nutritious, but when fed with steroid laden feed to tenderize their meat, then they can cause cancer. Therefore, the desi chicken is safer then eating a boiler. Many people in the west discard necks of the boilers because that is the point at which they are injected with steroids.

Eat only lean meat–have it grilled, baked or roasted. Avoid fast foods–it is high in cholesterol and low in all the nutrients.

Eat plenty of fibre, which is present in beans, grains, sprouts, unpeeled fruits and raw vegetables.

Stay off salted and fried foods when you are hungry, raw vegetables and fruits are better alternatives.

Eat only when you are relaxed and hungry, eat 2 hours before going to bed and eat 6 small meals per day instead of six large ones. Chew food thoroughly. Drink at least 12-15 glasses of water per day. Avoid cola drink, instead drink lassi, nimbu pani or coconut water. Avoid alcohol and too much coffee/tea, instead drink mint tea to which lime juice and honey has been added.

Cut down on white sugar, instead use natural sweetener like jaggery and honey.

Eat a variety of foods

Since no single food supplies all the nutrients to maintain a healthy body, eat a variety of foods and eat them in moderation. Always choose low calorie foods instead of high calorie ones. Eat plenty of fibre which not only helps in controlling body weight but also ensures body against many incurable diseases. Besides eat plenty of fruits (atleast 5 different types of fruits per day and gorge on vegetable salads. At least 50 percent of your food intake should be in the raw form. Raw food is full of antioxidants which fights diseases. Drink a glass of vegetable juice every day, it frees the body of toxins.

Don't miss on proteins, have 1 egg or 2 egg whites per day. Avoid red meat and go in for lean fish and chicken without the skin and if you are a vegetarian go in for soyabean products and sprouts.

Avoid too much fat

Consume less fat in the form of ghee, better, oil or cream. Too much fat increases the activity of free radicals in the body, if they are produced in excess then they cause ageing and increase blood cholesterol.

Maintain your ideal weight

Although there are no hard and fast rules about weight, you should maintain your weight in which you feel good. Stay away from junk and packaged foods and try to snack on popcorn, puffed rice, khakra, Marie biscuit or other low fat biscuits, cornflakes or crispies. Increase your physical activity, climb stairs instead of using the lift, park some distance away from your destination and walk, get off the bus a couple of stops before and walk.

Avoid too much sugar

Sugar is like white poison, people eating too much sugar not only fall victim to cancer but also acidity, depression, yeast infection, obesity, heart disease and diabetes. When sugarcane is converted into sugar, every known and unknown vitamin and mineral is removed from it except carbohydrates. The result is that the stomach has to draw vitamins, minerals and nutrients from other tissues to balance its metabolism. This sugar is very difficult to assimilate compared to other sugars such as fructose (found in fruits) or lactose (found in milk).

After you consume a lot of sugar (sucrose), the level of glucose in the blood rises rapidly, then also falls rapidly rather then remaining at a normal level. Excess sugar does not produce enough glycogen to keep blood sugar normal for long. This constant fluctuations in blood sugar levels give rise to lethargy, fatigue, headaches, migraine, insomnia and lack of energy. Sugar upsets the acid-alkali balance in the body; since our blood is mostly alkaline we should eat foods rich in minerals like potassium and sodium. This helps in maintaining bodies pH balance but sugar leaves residues of acidic acids in the body which gives rise to acidity.

Yeast infection also occurs due to excess intake of sugar; this infection mostly occurs due to overgrowth of the organism candida in the mouth, vagina and intestines. This disease is controlled by friendly bacteria, but sugar effects the normal working of bacteria, besides providing yeast with a sugar substratum on which to overgrow.

Heart disease is also triggered by sugar; sugar raises the cholesterol levels in the blood which gives birth to a heart attack. Since sugar is sweetest of all foods in the diet, so people eat far too much of it which not only causes tooth decay, but also diabetes in carbohydrate sensitive people.

Avoid too much salt

Common salt or sodium chloride is the bodies main source of sodium. Sodium is a very important mineral in the body, but excess of it can result in high blood pressure, circulatory problems, heart problems and kidney complaints. An average adult can consume about 3 grams of sodium per day. Sodium is also found in certain foods which use flavor enhancers like ajino-motto, soda bicarbonate and baking powder.

Do not miss breakfast

Missing breakfast can lead to overeating during lunch and dinner time, which is why you tend to turn obese. If you want to maintain your weight, eat a heavy breakfast because your metabolism is at its highest in the morning, it progressively tapers down as the day advances. Therefore, taking a lot of food during lunch and dinner can give you major calories which you are unable to burn during that time of the day.

Drink alcohol in moderation

If you like alcohol you can drink it in moderation. A little alcohol a peg or two does no harm to the body, but excess gives rise to many incurable diseases. In fact recent research has indicated that a glass of red wine per day is an excellent protection against heart disease.

Drink plenty of water

Water is the exhilarate of life. Every cell in our body depends upon water for its survival, without it we would die in a matter of few days. To maintain the proper amount of water in your body drink at least 8 to 10 glasses of water per day and more if you are physically active and sweat a lot. In hot weather you should take more water because large amounts of water are lost through perspiration. Pregnant women and nursing mothers should drink extra water to help maintain their milk supply. Infants too need water during hot weather, therefore babies should be offered water between their foods.

smooth paste, cover with silver foil and refreeze till firm.

Table 2.1
Optimum Weight Related to Height for Adults

Women				Men			
Height		Weight in kgs		Height		Weight in kgs	
Ft	Ins	Cms	Range	Ft	Ins	Cms	Range
4	10	147.3	43.5 – 48.5	5	0	152.4	50 – 55
4	11	149.9	44.5 – 49.9	5	1	154.8	52.2 – 57.7
5	0	152.4	45.8 – 51.3	5	2	157.5	53.5 – 58.5
5	1	154.9	47.2 – 52.6	5	3	160.0	54.9 – 60.3
5	2	157.5	48.5 – 54.0	5	4	162.6	56.2 – 61.7
5	3	160.0	49.9 – 55.3	5	5	165.1	57.6 – 63.0
5	4	162.6	51.3 – 57.2	5	6	167.6	59.0 – 64.9
5	5	165.1	52.6 – 59.0	5	7	170.2	60.8 – 66.7
5	6	167.6	54.4 – 61.2	5	8	172.7	62.6 – 68.9
5	7	170.2	56.2 – 63.0	5	9	175.3	64.4 – 70.8
5	8	172.7	57.1 – 64.9	5	10	177.8	66.2 – 72.6
5	9	175.3	59.9 – 66.7	5	11	180.3	68.0 – 74.8
5	10	177.8	61.7 – 68.5	6	0	182.9	69.9 – 77.1
5	11	180.3	63.5 – 70.3	6	1	185.4	71.7 – 79.4
6	0	182.9	65.3 – 72	6	2	188	73.5 – 81.6

Table 2.2
Calorie Content of Food*

Food	Calories per 100 gm edible portion	Food	Calories per 100 gm edible portion
Dairy Food		**Fish and Sea Food**	
Milk whole (Buffalo)	115	Bhetki (Khajura)	70-80
Milk whole (Cow)	65	Pomfret (White)	85
Milk Skimmed	30	Black Pomfrets (Halwa)	110
Butter milk	15	Salmon (Canned)	120
Curds	60	Rohu	95
Cheese (Ripened)	350	Tuna	290
Butter	720	Prawns	85
		Shrimps	85
Ghee & Oils		Ravas	112
Fats and Cooking oils	900	Sardomes	101
Ghee (Buffalo)	900	Mackarels	93
Ghee (Cow)	900	Lobster	90
Hydrogenated Cooking Oil	900	Sole	94
Ground-nut, corn, Coconut oils	900	**Pulses and Legumes**	
		Green gram (Mung)	334
Salad Dressings		Green gram dal (Mung Dal)	350
		Black gram (Urd Dal)	345
Mayonnaise	734	Bengal Gram Dal (Chana dal)	370
French	500	Lentil (Masur dal)	340
Meat and Poultry		Red gram (Tur dal)	335
		Rajmah beans	346
Mutton	190-195	Soya beans	432
Chicken	170		
Duck	326	**Vegetables**	
Beef	115	Cabbage	25
Pork	110	Cauliflower	30
Ham (Cooked)	400	Carrots	50
Egg (Hen)	170	Corn (Fresh)	30
Kidney (Sheep)	115	Coriander leaves	44
Liver (Sheep)	150	Cucumber	10

Food	Calories per 100 gm edible portion
Brinjals	24
Bitter gourd	25
Beetroots	45
Drumstick	25
Lady's finger (Bhindi)	35
Leeks	75
Lettuce leaves	20
Mint (Pudina)	50
Fenugreek (Methi ka sag)	50
French beans	26
Onions (Small)	60
Onions (Large)	50
Peas green (Fresh)	90
Potatoes	95
Sweet potatoes	120
Radish white (Muli)	15
Spinach (Palak)	25
Tomato (Fresh)	20
Tomato (Juice)	21
Tomato (Ketchup)	88
Fruits	
Apples	55-60
Apricots (Fresh)	53
Bananas (Ripe)	104
Bananas (Green)	110
Banana (Yellow variety)	120
Cherries (Red)	64
Currants (Black)	316
Coconut (Tender)	40
Dates (Khajur)	144
Figs	35
Grapes (Green variety)	70
Guava (Country)	50
Jack fruit	90
Lemon (Sour Lime)	40-50
Lemon (Sweet)	40
Lichees	60
Mango (Ripe)	75
Melon (Water)	15
Orange (Nagpur)	40
Orange (Juice)	9
Papaya (Ripe)	30
Peaches	50
Pineapple	45
Plums (Red)	50
Pomegranate	65
Raisins (Kishmish)	300
Pears	52
Seetaphal (Custard Apple)	100-115
Sapota (Chiku)	100-120
Strawberries	44
Sugar-cane	80
Sugar-cane juice	80
Grape-fruit	45
Grape-fruit juice	40
Cereal and Cereal Food	
Bajra	360
Barley	335
Jowar	350
Oatmeal	374
Rice, raw (Milled)	345
Rice, raw (Unmilled)	350
Vermicelli	350
Wheat flour (Whole - Atta)	340
Wheat flour (Refined-Maida)	350
Bread (White)	245
Bread (Brown)	244
Corn flakes	440
Biscuits (Sweet)	450
Biscuts (Salt)	534

Food	Calories per 100 gm edible portion	Food	Calories per 100 gm edible portion
Nuts & Seeds		**Alcoholic Beverages**	
Almond	655	Beer	78
Cashew Nuts	595	Gin	320
Coconut (Dry)	660	Rum	300-308
Ground-nuts (Roasted)	560	Whiskey	300-306
Pistachio Nuts	625	Vodka	280-285
Walnuts	685	Brandy	305
Apricots (Dried)	306	Wine (Dry)	135
Miscellaneous		Wine (Sweet)	150
Arrowroot flour	334	Toddy (Sweet)	59
Cocoa powder	430	Toddy (Fermented)	38
Honey	320	**Non-Alcoholic Beverages**	
Jaggery	380		
Sago	350		
Papads	300		
Jam	275	Carbonated drinks	0
Milk Chocolate	520	Carbonated soda	0
Coffee	440	Cola drinks (Sweetened)	40

*WHO release, 1986.

Table 2.3
Various Constituents of Food*
Protein, Fat, Carbohydrate and Fibre Content of Foods
(Per 100 gms edible portion)

Food 1	Protein (gm) 2	Fat (gm) 3	Carb. (gm) 4	Fibre (gm) 5
Dairy Foods				
Milk whole (Buffalo)	4.3	8.8	5.0	—
Milk whole (Cow)	3.2	4.0	4.4	—
Milk (Skimmed)	2.3	traces	5.0	—
Butter milk	0.8	1.1	0.5	—
Curds	3.1	4.0	3.0	—
Cheese (Ripened)	24.0	25.0	6.0	—
Butter	—	81.0	—	—
Fats and Cooking oils				
Ghee (Buffalo)	—	100	—	—
Ghee (Cow)	—	100	—	—
Hydrogenated Cooking Oil	—	100	—	—
Ground-nut, corn, coconut, Mustard	—	100	—	—
Salad Dressings				
Mayonnaise	trace	80	trace	—
French	trace	40	13.3	—
Meat and Poultry				
Mutton	18-19	13	0	0
Chicken	18	10	0	0
Duck	21.6	4.8	0	0
Beef	22.6	2.6	0	0
Pork	19	4.4	—	—
Egg (Hen)	13.3	13.3	—	—
Kidney (Sheep)	21.0	4	—	—
Liver (Sheep)	19.3	8	1.3	—
Ham (Cooked)	24	33	0	0

Food 1	Protein (gm) 2	Fat (gm) 3	Carb. (gm) 4	Fibre (gm) 5
Fish and Sea Food				
Bhetki	14	1	2	—
Pomfret	17	1.3	2	—
Black Pomfrets (Halwa)	20.3	1.3	2	—
Salmon (Canned)	17	5	0	0
Rohu	17	1.4	4.4	—
Tuna	24	21	0	—
Prawns	21	trace	0	—
Shrimps	17	trace	3	—
Ravas	22.2	1.1	3.3	—
Sardines	21	2	0	—
Mackarels	19	2	0	—
Lobster	2n1	1	0	—
Sole	16.2	2.3	2.2	—
Pulses and Legumes				
Green gram (Mung)	24	1.3	57	4.1
Green gram dal (Mung Dal)	24.5	1.2	60	0.8
Black gram (Urd Dal)	24	1.4	60	0.9
Bengal Gram Dal (Chanadal)	21	5.6	60	1.2
Lentil (Masur dal)	25.1	0.7	59	0.7
Red gram (Tur dal)	22.3	1.7	58	1.5
Rajmah beans	23	1.3	61	—
Soya beans	43.2	19.5	21	3.7
Vegetables				
Cabbage	2	trace	5	1
Cauliflower	2.6	0.4	4	1.2
Carrots	1	0.2	10.6	1.2
Coriander leaves	3.3	0.6	6.3	1.2
Cucumber	0.4	0.1	2.5	0.4
Brinjals	1.4	0.3	4	1.3
Bitter gourd	1.6	0.2	4.2	0.8
Drumstick	2.5	0.1	3.7	5
Lady's finger (Bhindi)	2	0.2	6.4	1.2

Food 1	Protein (gm) 2	Fat (gm) 3	Carb. (gm) 4	Fibre (gm) 5
Leeks	1.8	0.1	17.2	1.3
Lettuce leaves	2.1	0.3	2.5	0.5
Mint (Pudina)	4.8	0.6	6	2
Fenugreek leaves (Methi Ka Sag)	4.4	0.9	6	1.1
French beans	1.7	0.1	4.5	1.8
Beet root	1.7	0.1	8.8	1
Onions (Small)	1.8	0.1	12.6	0.6
Onions (Mature)	1.2	0.1	11.1	0.6
Peas green (Fresh)	7.2	0.1	16	4
Potatoes (Alu)	1.6	0.1	22.6	0.4
Sweet potatoes	1.2	0.3	28.2	0.8
Radish white (Muli)	0.7	0.1	3.4	0.8
Spinach (Palak)	2	0.7	3.0	0.6
Tomato (Fresh)	1	0.2	3.6	0.8
Tomato (Juice)	0.8	trace	4.1	0.25
Tomato (Ketchup)	trace	trace	23.5	trace
Fruits				
Apples	0.2	0.5	13.4	1.0
Apricots (Fresh)	1	0.3	11.6	1
Bananas (Ripe)	1.2	0.3	27.2	0.4
Bananas (Green)	1	1	28	—
Cherries (Red)	1	0.5	13.8	0.4
Currants (Black)	2.7	0.5	75.2	1
Coconut (Tender)	1	1	6	—
Dates (Fresh)	1.2	0.4	34.0	4
Figs	1.3	0.2	7.6	2.2
Grapes (Green variety)	0.5	0.3	16.5	3
Guava (Country)	1	0.3	11.2	5.2
Jack fruit	2	0.3	20	1
Lemon (Sour Lime)	1	1	8	2
Lemon (Sweet)	0.7	0.3	7.3	0.7
Lichees	1.4	0.3	14	0.2
Mango (Ripe)	0.6	0.4	16.9	0.7
Melon (Water)	0.2	0.2	3.3	0.2

Food 1	Protein (gm) 2	Fat (gm) 3	Carb. (gm) 4	Fibre (gm) 5
Orange	0.7	0.2	10.9	0.3
Orange (Juice)	0.2	0.1	2	—
Peaches	1.2	0.3	10.5	1.2
Papaya (Ripe)	0.6	0.1	7.2	0.8
Pears	0.6	0.2	11.9	1.0
Pineapple	0.4	0.1	10.8	0.5
Plums (Red)	0.7	0.5	11.1	0.4
Pomegranate	1.6	0.1	14.5	5.1
Raisins (Kishmish)	1.8	0.3	74.6	1.1
Seetaphal (Custard Apple)	1.6	0.4	23.5	3.1
Sapota (Chiku)	0.7	1.1	21.4	2.6
Strawberries	0.7	0.2	10	11
Sugar-cane	trace	0	20	3
Sugar-cane juice	trace	0	20	3
Cereal and Cereal Food				
Bajra	11.6	5	68	1
Barley	11.5	1.3	19.6	4
Jowar	10.4	2	72.6	1.6
Oatmeal	13.6	7.6	63	3.5
Rice, raw (Milled)	7	0.5	78.2	0.2
Rice, raw (Unmilled)	7.5	1.0	76.7	0.6
Vermicelli	9	trace	78	trace
Wheat flour (Whole - Atta)	12.1	1.7	69.4	2
Wheat flour (Refined-Maida)	11	1	74	0.3
Bread (White)	7.8	0.7	52	0.2
Wheat germ	29.2	7.4	53.3	1.4
Bread (Brown)	9	1.4	49.50	1.2
Biscuits (Sweet)	6.4	15.2	72	—
Biscuts (Salt)	6.6	32.4	54.6	—
Nuts & Seeds				
Almond	21	59	11	2
Cashew Nuts	21	47	22	1
Coconut (Dried)	7	62	18	7
Ground-nuts (Roasted)	32	40	19	3

Food 1	Protein (gm) 2	Fat (gm) 3	Carb. (gm) 4	Fibre (gm) 5
Pistachio Nuts	20	54	16	2
Walnuts	16	65	11	3
Miscellaneous				
Arrowroot flour	0	0	83	—
Cocoa powder	20	25	30	—
Honey	0.3	0	79.5	—
Jaggery	1.5	0.3	86.1	—
Sago	0.2	0.2	87.1	—
Papads	19	0.3	52.4	—
Jam	0	0	70	—
Milk Chocolate	3.6	10.7	79	trace
Coffee	trace	5	5	—
Tea (Leaves)	8	4	70	6
Non-Alcoholic Beverages				
Carbonated drinks	0	0	0	—
Carbonated soda	0	0	0	—
Cola drinks (Sweetened)	0	0	11	—

*WHO release, 1986.

Table 2.4
Distilled Alcoholic Beverages*

Distilled spirits, liquors or spirits	Usual portion in ml	Approximate calorie value of usual portion	Approximate calorie value of 100 ml
Brandy	20	60	305
Gin	20	75	365
Rum	50	160	325
Vodka	50	295	590
Whisky	50	150	305
Fortified and Aromatic Wines			
Port	30	55	180
Sherry dry	30	40	140
Sherry sweet	30	45	150
Vermouth	105	170	160
Sparklng Wines			
Champagne	135	120	90
Fermented malt Beverages			
Beer or ale—lager or brown	250	100	40
Beer strong	250	195	80
Toddy (Country Beer)	250	140	65

*Who release, 1986.

(Calories vary depending on alcohol content and natural sugars, Vitamins B1, B2, B7 and C are also present in toddy)

1gm of Alcohol (about 1.16 ml) = 7.1 cals.

Table 2.5
Calories Spent in Various Physical Activities*

Activity	Cal / min	Activity	Cal / min
Standing	2.6	Skating : Recreational	5
Driving a car leisurely	2.8	Vigorous	15
Walking indoors	3.1	Badminton	
Taking shower (with water at room temp.)	3.4	Recreational	5.2
		Competitive	10
Dressing	3.4	Basketball	6.9
Cleaning windows	3.7	Tennis : Recreational	7
Sweeping floors	3.9	Competitive	11
Ironing clothes	4.2	Soccer	9.0
Gardening	4.7	Mountain climbing	10.0
Pick-and-shovel work	6.7	Judo and Karate	13.0
Chopping wood	7.5	Wrestling	14
Digging earth	8.6	Swimming: Pleasure	6.0
Walking up-stairs	8-15	Competitive	10-12
Playing volleyball:		Dancing : Moderate	5.0
Recreational	3.5	Walking (3.5 mph)	5.6-7.0
Competitive	8.0	up-hill (3.5 mph)	15
Golf: Foursome — Twosome	3.7-5.0	Running	
Table-tennis	4.9-7.0	12 min./mile	10.0
Rowing: Recreational	5	8 min./mile	15.0
Competitive	15	6 min./mile	20.0
Cycling : 5 to 15 miles/hr	5-12	5 min./mile	25.0

*Sharkey B. J., Physiological Fitness and Weight Control, Mountain Press Publishing Co., Missoula, Mont., 1974

Chapter 3

JUICES

Tomato and Orange Juice Cocktail

2 cups orange juice.
4 cups tomato juice.
Mint leaves.
Chopped orange flesh.

Chill the juices thoroughly with a few bruised mint leaves. Serve in small glasses topped with orange flesh.

Banana Coconut Milk Shake

1 cup coconut milk.
1 small banana. 1 tblsp.
honey. 4 seeded dates.

Blend all the above ingredients in the blender till smooth. Serve well chilled.

Carrot Juice Cocktail

Juice of 1 kilo carrots. Mix with glucose, salt, pepper and

grounded cumin seeds. Serve chilled. If you like you can use half carrot juice and half milk combination, but then omit the glucose and spices.

Carrot and Apple Cocktail

1-1/2 cups carrot juice.

½ cup Apple juice.

1 tsp. honey.

Mix together all the above ingredients and serve cold.

Carrot and Spinach Cooler

3 cups carrot juice.

¼ cup each of celery and spinach juice.

Salt to taste.

Mix all the above ingredients and serve chilled.

Citrus Punch

1 lime, 1 lemon, 1 orange.

1 tblsp. honey.

1 tblsp. each of pineapple.

cherry and orange bits.

Squeeze juice from fruits. Mix in honey and chill. Decorate with fruit bits.

Pineapple Punch

2-1/2 cups pineapple juice.

½ cup orange juice.

2 tblsp. honey.

2 tblsps. chopped pineapple.

Mix the juices with honey and chill. Decorate with pineapple bits.

Tomato Juice Cocktail

Chill tomato juice and season with salt and lime juice and pepper powder.

Orange Punch

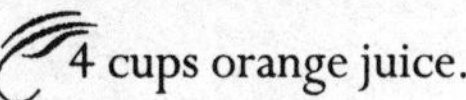

4 cups orange juice.

½ cup lemon juice.

4 tblsps. honey.

2 tblsps. chopped orange meat.

1 tblsp. chopped mint.

Mix honey with juices. Chill and decorate with mint and orange meat.

Pomegranate Cooler

4 cups pomegranate juice.

2 cups orange juice.

Glucose, salt and pepper to taste.

2 tblsps. chopped orange meat.

Mix together the juices, spices and glucose. chill and serve; decorate with orange meat.

Watermelon Cooler

4 cups watermelon juice.

2 cups sweet lime juice.

Glucose, salt and pepper to taste.

4 tblsps. chopped watermelon.

Mix together juices and spices. Chill and serve decorated with watermelon pieces.

Orange Cooler

2 large oranges, peeled and sliced.

2 tblsps. honey.

2 cups crushed ice.

1 cup water.

Mix oranges and water and blend in the blender for 25 seconds, then add honey and ice; mix for further 25 seconds. Sieve and served chilled.

Pineapple Cooler

2 lemons, peeled and sliced.

2 slices pineapple.

1 cup water.

4 tblsps. honey.

2 cups crushed ice.

Blend the above ingredients in the blender for ½ a minute. Sieve and serve topped with bruised mint leaves.

Grape Cooler

250 grams seedless grapes.

1 peeled and sliced orange.

1 peeled and sliced lemon.

1 cup water.

2 tblsps. honey.

Blend all the above ingredients in the blender. Sieve and serve chilled.

Lemon Cooler

2 large lemons, peeled and cut.

1 glass chilled water.

4 tblsps. honey.

2 cups crushed ice.

Blend together water and lemon in the blender for 25 seconds. Sieve and put in the blender along with the remaining ingredients. Chill and serve.

Strawberry Cooler

1 cup orange juice.

2 cups strawberries.

4 tblsps. honey.

1 cup crushed ice.

Blend all the above ingredients in the blender till smooth. Serve well chilled.

Cherry Crush

½ cup pineapple juice.

½ cup fresh stoned cherries.

1 small pealed and sliced lemon.

2 tblsps. almonds.

2 tblsps. honey.

2 cups crushed ice.

Mix all the above ingredients together in the blender and blend for ½ minute.

Pineapple and Cucumber Refresher

1 cup pineapple juice.

2 tsps. lemon juice.

1 cup diced cucumber.

1 cup crushed ice.

Blend all the above ingredients in the blender till smooth. Serve chilled.

Tomato Refresher

500 grams tomatoes.

1 cup chipped celery.

1 sprig parsley.

1 small onion.

Put in the juicer and extract juice. Serve with salt and pepper, very cold.

Chapter 4

SOUPS

Carrot Soup

2 cups diced carrots
100 grams tomatoes
1 small onion, minced
¼ cup boiled peas
1 tablespoon cornflour mixed in
¼ cup skimmed milk
1 sprig parsley or ajmood
Salt and pepper to taste

Cook together tomatoes, carrot and onion. When soft pass through a sieve. Reheat and mix in the cornflour. Cook till thick. Sprinkle salt and pepper on top and decorate it with peas and parsley.

Chicken and Sweet Corn Soup

1 cup canned and creamed corn
5 cups either mutton or chicken stock, i.e.
liquor made by boiling (stewing) bones
1 egg white lightly beaten
1-½ tablespoon cornflour

2 tablespoons shredded cooked chicken

¼ teaspoon monosodium glutamate i.e. Japanese salt ajinomotto

Salt and pepper to taste

Mix cornflour with 6 tablespoons water to a smooth paste. Bring stock to boiling; add corn and simmer for 5 minutes. Add cornflour and seasonings and cook till the soup thickens. Add lightly beaten egg-white and keep stirring all the time. Decorate with chicken and parsley.

Summer Fruit Soup

500 grams cooking apples, pears

250 grams peaches

A few whole strawberries for decoration

¾ litre water

Strained juice of 2 limes

100 grams sugar

A big pinch of powdered cinnamom

Put the sliced fruits along with water in a pan and cook till soft. Pass through a sieve. Dissolve 2 teaspoons cornflour in ¼ cup water and put it into the fruits along with sugar. Cook till it gets thick. Chill and decorate with either strawberries or cherries.

Cheese and Vegetable Soup

4 large tomatoes, peeled and pureed i.e., strained through a sieve

50 grams paneer, sliced into tiny pieces

100 grams mixed vegetables like carrots, french-beans

1 sprig celery

1 litre water mixed with

1 tablespoon monosodium glutamate or ajinomotto

1 tablespoon cornflour dissolved in ¼ cup water

Put tomatoes in water and cook for 5 minutes. Cut the vegetables into tiny pieces and put into the tomatoes. Boil till it is crisp tender. Add paneer and cornflour and cook till it is slightly thick. Serve hot.

Vegetable and Chicken Soup

½ cup shredded cooked lean chicken
250 grams mixed vegetables like cabbage, carrot, french-beans and peas
1 cup pureed tomatoes i.e. boiled, crushed and passed through a sieve
1 tablespoon cornflour dissolved in ¼ cup skimmed milk
6 tablespoons chickenstock
Salt and pepper to taste

Mix together stock, tomato and vegetables. Boil till the vegetables are tender crisp. Mix in chicken and the flour mixture and cook till the soup thickens a little. Add salt and pepper and serve hot with a pat of butter.

Tomato and Cheese Soup

4 large tomatoes, peeled and pureed
50 grams shredded chicken
50 grams paneer, cut into tiny pieces
1 litre chicken stock
1-½ tablespoon soya sauce
1-½ tablespoon vinegar
1 tablespoon cornflour dissolved in ¼ cup water
1 teaspoon monosodium glutamate i.e. ajinomotto
Salt and pepper to taste

Put tomatoes in the stock and cook for 5 minutes. Add the rest of the ingredients and cook till the soup thickens. Serve hot.

Chapter 5

VEGETABLES

French Bean Bhaji

1 cup shredded French beans.

1 small onion, minced.

¼ tsp. each of grated ginger and garlic.

1 big tomato.

2-inch piece coconut.

¼ tsp. mustard seeds.

Handful of coriander leaves.

2 green chilies, minced.

¼ tsp. turmeric powder.

A pinch of chili powder. Salt to taste.

Grind coconut, ginger, garlic and onion. Heat 1 tsp. oil and put mustard seeds, when they stop popping, add grounded paste and fry till the raw taste disappears. Put in all the remaining ingredients and cook till the beans are done.

Corn Treat

½ cup each of boiled corn and peas.

1 boiled potato, peeled and diced.

1-½ curd made of skimmed milk.

Handful of coriander leaves.

2 green chilies, minced.

A big pinch garam masala.

¼ tsp. cumin seeds.

4 tblsps. tamrind juice mixed with 1 tblsp. sugar.

A big pinch each of pepper and chili powder.

Salt to taste.

Mix together vegetables with salt and chilies. Pour curd on top, add tamrind, sprinkle spices and roasted cumin seeds and decorate with coriander leaves.

Spinach with Vegetables

1 cup chopped spinach.

250 grams mixed vegetables of your choice.

100 grams tomatoes, chopped.

1 onion, minced. ½ tsp.

minced ginger and garlic.

2 green chiles, minced.

¼ tsp. turmeric powder.

A pinch of chili powder.

Salt to taste.

Mix together all the above ingredients with the exception of garlic and ginger and cook over a slow fire till soft. Mash to a paste, add half cup water blended with half teaspoon flour and cook till thick. Heat 1 tsp. oil and fry garlic and ginger and put over the vegetables.

Pumpkin Bhajee

1 cup sliced pumpkin.

1 medium tomato, pureed.

¼ tsp. each of grated ginger and garlic.

1 small onion, minced.

¼ tsp. cumin seeds.

Pinch of pepper powder.

Salt to taste.

Heat 1 tsp. oil and add cumin seeds, when they stop tossing, put in the remaining ingradients and cook over a slow fire till soft.

Vegetable Stew

250 grams mixed vegetables like French beans, carrots, peas, and cauliflower and ladies fingers.

100 grams tomatoes. 1 tsp.

grated ginger, ¼ tsp.

turmeric powder and cumin seeds.

2 green chilies.

A few coriander leaves.

Banana Thoran

2 raw bananas, peeled and diced.

¼ coconut grated.

2 green chilies.

2 small onions.

¼ tsp. turmeric powder.

2 flakes garlic.

¼ tsp. each of cumin and mustard seeds.

A few curry leaves.

Salt to taste.

A pinch of chili powder.

Grind together coarsely coconut, chilies, onion, garlic and cumin seeds. Cook bananas in little water and salt till tender and dry. Add coconut and curry leaves and mix nicely. Heat 1 tsp. oil and add mustard, when the seeds stop popping put over the thoran.

Potato Bhajee

1 potato, boiled, peeled and diced.

2-inch piece coconut.

1 green chili, minced.

1 small green portion.

Handful of chopped coriander leaves.

A big pinch chili powder.

Salt and lime juice to taste.

Grind coconut, set little aside and extract milk from the rest. Mix together all the above ingredients with the exception of grounded coconut and coriander leaves. Decorate with coconut and coriander leaves.

Mustard Potatoes

½ tsp. mustard seeds.

1 big potato, boiled, peeled and diced.

2 green chilies, minced.

¼ tsp. each of grated garlic and ginger handful of coriander leaves.

Salt to taste.

Heat 1 tsp. oil and fry mustard seeds, add ginger and garlic and fry lightly; remove from fire and mix in the remaining ingredients.

Brinjal Pachadi

1 cup curd made of skimmed milk.

1 small purple brinjal.

1 green chili, minced.

A big pinch each of mustard seeds and urad dal.

Handful of coriander leaves.

1 red chili broken.

Salt to taste.

Bake the brinjal over a gas flame till the skin turns black and wrinkled. Toss into the cold water. Peel the skin and mash the pulp to a paste. Mix with curd along with salt, chilies and coriander leaves. Heat half teaspoon of oil and put in mustard, red chili and dal; when the seeds stop popping, put into the curds.

Palak Paneer

100 grams paneer, cubed.

1 cup chopped spinach.

1 small onion.

½ inch piece ginger.

1 green chili.

1 medium tomato.

2 flakes garlic, crushed.

A big pinch chili powder.

¼ tsp. turmeric powder.

Salt to taste.

Put spinach to cook with all the above ingredients with the exception of paneer and garlic. When it is tender, mash, put in ½ cup water along with paneer. Cook for 5 minutes. Heat 1 tsp. oil and fry garlic and put over the palak paneer.

Garlic Bhindi

250 grams ladies fingers.

10 flakes garlic made into paste.

50 grams tomatoes, chopped.

½ tsp. turmeric powder.

¼ tsp. each of chili and coriander powder.

Salt to taste.

Make a slit in the center of each bhindi. Mix together all the spices and garlic, fill into each bhindi. Heat 1 tsp. oil and put in the bhindi; after a few minutes add tomatoes and salt. Cook over a slow fire till done.

Carrots in Fenugreek Leaves

250 grams carrots, chopped.

1 cup sliced methi or fenugreek leaves.

1 medium tomato, chopped.

2 green chilies, minced.

½ tsp. each of ginger and garlic paste.

¼ tsp. turmeric powder.

A big pinch chili powder.

Salt to taste.

Heat 1 tsp. oil and add ginger and garlic; fry till soft; add carrots and fry for a few minutes; put in the remaining ingredients and cook till the vegetables are done. Do not add water.

Mixed Vegetable Bhajee

1 medium potato, peeled and chopped. 100 grams cauliflower, chopped.

1 carrot, chopped.

½ cup green peas.

½ tsp. grated ginger.

½ tsp. cumin seeds.

Handful of coriander leaves.

50 grams tomatoes, chopped.

¼ tsp. turmeric powder.

Big pinch chili powder.

Salt to taste.

Heat 1 tsp. oil and add cumin seeds, when they stop popping, add all the above ingredients and cook without adding water till done.

Spinach Delight

½ cup chopped spinach.

¼ cup skimmed milk.

½ tsp. minced ginger.

1 green chili, minced.

¼ tsp. powdered cumin seeds.

Salt to taste.

Cook the spinach with all the above ingredients with the exception of milk. When tender and dry, mash to a paste, put in milk, reheat and serve.

Drumstick Bhaji

2 drumsticks, scraped and diced.

½ tsp. grated ginger.

¼ tsp. cumin seeds.

A big pinch each of turmeric powder and garam masala.

1 medium tomato.

Handful of coriander leaves.

4 tblsp. skimmed milk.

2 tblsp. tomato ketchup.

A big pinch chili powder.

Salt to taste.

Heat 1 tsp. oil and add cumin seeds and ginger. When the seeds stop popping, put in the tomatoes and all the spices and cook till soft. Mix in the remaining ingredients and cook till tender and almost dry.

Methi Paneer

100 grams paneer, cubed.

1 cup fenugreek leaves or methi, sliced.

½ tsp. each of garlic and ginger, grounded.

¼ tsp. turmeric powder.

2 green chilies, minced.

1 big tomato, chopped.

Salt to taste.

A big pinch chili powder.

Heat 1 tsp. oil and add ginger and garlic. Cook till soft. Add the remaining ingredients without adding paneer. Cook till dry, put in paneer and cook for a few minutes more.

Paneer Burji

100 grams paneer, crumbled, 1 small onion, minced.

1 big tomato, chopped.

¼ tsp. each of turmeric powder and cumin seeds.

½ tsp. ginger, grated.

1 green chili, minced.

Handful of chopped coriander leaves.

A big pinch chili powder.

Salt to taste.

Heat 1 tsp. oil and add onion, ginger and chili and cook till soft. Add the remaining ingredients and cook till dry.

Vegetable Palak

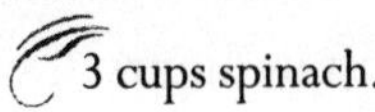

3 cups spinach.

½ cup each of dill, methi and khatti palak.

100 grams sliced pumpkin.

100 grams white gourds, scraped and diced.

100 grams carrots.

1 medium potato.

200 grams tomatoes.

8 green chilies.

¼ cup coriander leaves.

1 tblsp. dhania jeera powder.

¼ tsp. turmeric powder.

1-inch piece minced ginger.

1 tsp. cumin seeds.

Salt and chili powder to taste.

Heat 4 tblsp. ghee and put in all the above ingredients with the exception of ginger and cumin seeds. Cover and cook without adding water till the mixture is cooked. Mash coarsely and reheat. Cook till thickish. Put in a serving dish. Fry cumin seeds and ginger in 1 tblsp. ghee and pour over the vegetables. Serve hot.

Black Palak

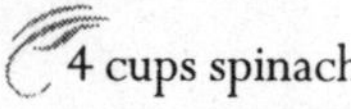

4 cups spinach.

1 cup each of methi and dill.

1 big brinjal, diced.

50 grams tomatoes.

1 tblsp. dhania jeera powder.

Salt and chili powder to taste.

Heat 4 tblsps. ghee and put in all the above ingredients. Cook without adding water till soft. Mash to a smooth paste. Reheat before serving.

Sersoan ka Sag

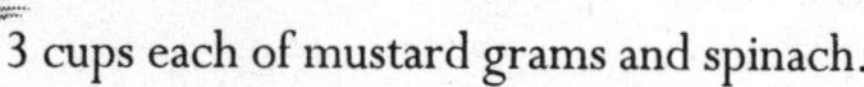

3 cups each of mustard grams and spinach.

4 green chilies, minced 1 tblsp.

Flour dissolved in ¼ cup water.

½ inch piece ginger, minced, 1 big tomato, diced.

1 tblsp. dhania jeera powder.

¼ tsp. turmeric powder.

Salt and chili powder to taste.

Mix together all the above ingredients with the exception of flour. Cook without adding water till the greens are soft. Mash to a paste and pass through a fine sieve. Reheat and put in the flour mixture. Cook till thickish. Pour 4 tblsp. of hot pure ghee on top and serve with makai-ki-roti. Turn to section on Indian Breads for recipe of makai-ki-roti.

Chapter 6

DALS & PULSES

Sprouted Brown Channa

250 grams sptouted brown channas, boiled.

¼ cup grounded coconut.

2 medium tomatoes, diced.

1 big onion; 5 flakes garlic.

1-inch piece ginger.

2 red chilies.

1 tblsp. dhania jeera powder.

1/8 tsp. garam masala.

A few coriander leaves.

Salt to taste.

Grind onion, ginger, garlic and red chilies to a paste. Heat 4 tblsps. oil, add 1 tsp. cumin seeds, when they stop popping, fry the grounded paste along with coconut, spices and salt. When well fried add tomatoes. When the oil floats to the top, mix in the channas; add 1 cup water and cook for 5 minutes. Decorate with coriander.

Sprouted Moong Dal Delight

200 grams sprouted moong dal.

¼ cup thick coconut juice.

1 big tomato sliced.

1 big onion, minced.

2 green chilies, minced, 1 tsp. grated ginger.

¼ tblsp. dhania jeera powder.

¼ tsp. turmeric powder.

Salt and chili powder to taste.

Grind onion, ginger and chilies to a paste. Heat 4 tblsps. oil and add mustard; when it stops tossing, put in onion paste and fry to a soft brown colour. Mix in dal and 2 cups water. Cook till the dal is tender. Heat 3 tblsps. oil and put in the coconut, fry and add the curd and all the spices. When the oil separates add the dal and carrots. Mix well and serve decorated with coriander.

Sprouted Moong Dal Special

200 grams sprouted moong dal.

¼ cup thick coconut juice.

1 big tomato sliced.

1 big onion, minced.

2 green chilies, minced.

1 tsp. grated ginger.

¼ tblsp. dhania jeera powder.

¼ tsp. turmeric powder.

Salt and chili powder to taste.

Boil the dal. Heat 4 tblsps. oil and add 1 tsp. cumin seeds. When they stop tossing, add onion and ginger and chilies along with spices and salt and cook till soft. Add tomato, when the oil separates mix in the dal. Add coconut milk. Bring to simmering point, decorate with chopped coriander leaves.

Sprouted Gram Pullao

2 cups Delhi rice.

1 cup sprouted gram, boiled.

1 large onion.

6 flakes garlic.

½ inch piece ginger.

4 green chilies.

½ cup coriander leaves.

Cardamoms.

¼ tsp. cumin seeds.

¼ tsp. turmeric powder.

Salt and chili powder to taste.

For decoration :

1 medium tomato, cut into strips.

4 green chilies, slatted.

Handful of coriander leaves.

A few fried cashew nuts.

Grind onion, ginger, garlic, chilies and coriander to a coarse paste. Heat 4 tblsps. oil and add all the whole spices. When the seeds stop popping, put in the channas, all the spices, salt and rice. Add enough water to stand 1-inch above the level of the rice. Cook till the rice is tender and dry. Fry tomato, coriander and chilies in 2 tblsps. oil and put over rice along with cashew nuts, serve at once.

Chole Aloo

1 cup white grams or kabuli chana.

1 medium potato, boiled peeled and diced, 1 big tomato, pureed.

½ - inch piece ginger, cut into strips, Handful of chopped coriander leaves.

2 green chilies, slatted.

¼ tsp. turmeric powder.

¼ tsp. packaged chola masala and cumin seeds.

Salt to taste.

Soak grams whole night in water, next morning boil the chana with a pinch of soda added to it. Drain out the water. Mash half the cholas. Heat ½ tsp. oil and add tomatoes and all the spices. Cook till dry, add salt, grams and potatoes. Add little water and cook for 5 minutes, heat ½ tsp. oil and fry cumin seeds, put over the channa and decorate with chilies, coriander and ginger.

Rajmah

1 cup rajmah or red kidney beans.

1 medium tomato, pureed.

½ tsp. ginger paste.

¼ tsp. turmeric powder.

2 green chilies, slitted, handful of chopped coriander leaves.

A big pinch chili powder.

¼ cup coconut milk.

Salt to taste.

Soak the beans whole night in water. Next morning boil them with a pinch of soda. Drain out the water. Heat ½ tsp. oil and add tomatoes, when soft add the remaining ingredients with the exception of coconut milk, cumin seeds and coriander leaves. Cook for 5 minutes, put in the milk and remove from fire. Fry cumin seeds in ½ tsp. of oil and put over the rajmah. Decorate with coriander leaves.

Channa Masaledar

1 cup black channa.

1 potato, boiled, peeled and diced.

Handful of chopped coriander leaves, 2 green chilies, minced.

1 small tomato, chopped.

1 small onion, minced, a pinch of chili powder and chat masala.

Salt to taste.

Soak chana whole night in water. Next morning boil with a pinch of soda, drain out the water and mix with potato and spices. Put on top tomato, onion, chilies and coriander leaves.

Mixed Pulse Usal

1 cup each of sprouted green mung, green and brown grams, soya beans and peas.

50 grams pureed tomatoes, 1 tsp.

grated ginger.

Handful of chopped coriander leaves.

2 green chilies, minced.

¼ tsp. cumin seeds.

¼ tsp. turmeric powder.

A few curry leaves.

2 tblsps. grated coconut.

A big pinch chili powder.

Salt to taste.

Steam cook all the sprouted grams and beans. Grind together ginger, chilies, coriander, coconut and curry leaves. Heat 1 tsp. oil and add cumin seeds, when the seeds stop popping add grounded paste, fry nicely and then add tomatoes, when dry add the beans and cook for few more minutes.

Mung Dal

1 cup mung dal yellow coloured.

¼ tsp. turmeric powder.

100 grams tomatoes.

Salt to taste.

Cook the dal till soft. Mash to a paste. Add pureed tomatoes along with salt and turmeric. Cook till tomatoes are cooked. Serve decorated with coriander leaves.

Lasuni Dal

1 cup masur dal.

4 flakes garlic, crushed to a paste.

¼ tsp. cumin seeds.

¼ tsp. turmeric powder.

Salt to taste.

Cook the dal along with salt and turmeric powder till soft. Mash to a paste. Heat 1 tsp. oil and fry garlic and cumin seeds and put over the dal.

Hingwali Dal

1 cup toovar dal.

1 medium tomato, peeled and pureed.

Handful of chopped coriander leaves.

A big pinch hing.

¼ tsp. cumin seeds.

¼ tsp. turmeric powder.

Salt to taste.

Cook the dal with tomatoes, salt and turmeric powder, mash to a paste. Add coriander leaves. Heat 1 tsp. oil and fry cumin seeds and hing and put over the dal.

Cocum Wali Dal

1 cup toovar dal.

5 to 6 cocums.

A big pinch hing.

2 green chilies, slitted.

½ tsp. grated ginger.

Handful of coriander leaves.

¼ tsp. turmeric powder.

A few curry leaves.

¼ tsp. each of mustard and cumin seeds.

Salt to taste.

Boil the dal till soft. Mash to a paste, add 2 cups water along with the rest of the ingredients with the exception of hing, mustard and cumin seeds. When the cocums turn soft heat 1 tsp. oil and fry the seeds and hing and put over the dal.

Masalewali Dal

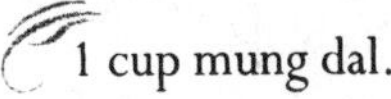

1 cup mung dal.

1 small onion, minced.

½ tsp. each of grated ginger and garlic.

2 green chilies, minced.

50 grams grated tomatoes.

A few curry leaves.

Handful of coriander leaves.

A pinch of garam masala.

Salt to taste.

Cook dal till soft. Heat 1 tblsp. oil and add cumin seeds. When the seeds stop tossing add onion, ginger, garlic and chilies, cook till soft, add tomatoes, when dry add dal, remove from fire after few minutes and sprinkle on top garam masala and coriander leaves.

Makhini Dal

1 cup mung dal.

1 small onion, minced.

1 small tomato, minced.

¼ tsp. grated ginger.

1 green chili, minced.

¼ tsp. turmeric powder.

Handful of coriander leaves.

¼ tsp. cumin seeds.

A big pinch of pepper and chili powder and mango powder.

Cook the dal in little water along with salt and turmeric till tender and dry. Each grain should remain separate. Sprinkle on top all the spices. Heat 1 tblsp. oil and add cumin seeds, when seeds stop popping, add tomato, ginger, chili, onion and coriander leaves, fry lightly and put over the dal.

Chapter 7

CHUTNEYS

Garlic chutney

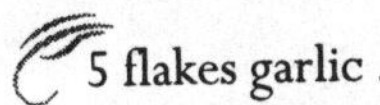

5 flakes garlic .

½ cup coriander leaves.

5 green chilies.

2-inch piece ginger.

Juice of 2 large limes.

Salt to taste.

Grind together all the above ingredients.

Tomato Chutney

2 medium raw green tomatoes.

4 green chilies.

1 tblsp. grated ginger.

1 cup coriander leaves.

Salt and lime juice to taste.

Grind together all the above ingredients.

Date Chutney

100 grams seedless dates.

3 green chilies.

1 tsp. cumin seeds.

½ cup coriander leaves.

Juice and pulp of 1 large lime.

Salt to taste.

Grind together all the above ingredients.

Groundnut Chutney

1 cup roasted groundnuts.

2 red and 2 green chilies.

½ cup coriander leaves.

3 flakes garlic.

8 mint leaves.

3 tblsps. lime juice.

Salt to taste.

Grind all the above ingredients together.

Sweet Chutney

1 lime-sized ball of tamrind.

12 seedless dates.

25 grams raisins.

12 cashewnuts.

1 tsp. cumin seeds.

Salt to taste.

Grind together all the above ingredients together.

Black Grape Chutney

50 grams black dried grapes.

1-inch piece ginger.

Juice of half lime.

2 green chilies.

Salt to taste.

Grind all the above ingredients to a paste.

Tamrind Chutney

12 seedless dates.

1 tblsp. grated jaggery.

4 tblsps. tamrind pulp.

1 tsp. cumin seeds.

1-inch piece ginger.

Salt to taste.

Grind together all the above ingredients to a paste.

Coriander and Dal Chutney

2 cups coriander leaves.

4 green chillies.

4 flakes garlic.

2 tblsps. soaked channa dal.

Lime juice and salt to taste.

Grind all the above ingredients to a paste.

Onion and Coriander Chutney

2 onions.

1 cup coriander leaves.

¼ cup mint leaves.

Juice of 1 lime.

8 flakes garlic.

Salt to taste.

Grind all the above ingredients to a paste.

Green Onion Chutney

6 medium green onions.

1 cup mint leaves.

4 green chilies.

½ cup coriander leaves.

2 tblsps. pomegranate seeds.

Juice of 1 lime.

Salt to taste.

Grind all the above ingredients to a paste.

Mint Chutney

1 cup mint leaves.

2 small onions.

2 green chilies.

1 green tomato.

2 tblsps. pomegranate seeds.

1 tblsp. lime juice.

Salt to taste.

Grind together all the above ingredients.

Reddish and Mango Chutney

1 big reddish with leaves.

1 medium raw mango.

Tender leaves of reddish.

½ cup coriander leaves.

Salt to taste.

Grind all the above ingredients to a paste.

Carrot and Coconut Chutney

100 grams carrots, peelad and grated.
2 green chilies.
1 tblsp. tamrind pulp.
2 tblsps. grated coconut.

Grind all the above ingredients to a paste.

Tomato and Mint Chutney

100 grams red tomatoes.
1 tsp. grated ginger.
2 green chilies.
½ cup each of mint and coriander leaves.
1 tblsp. lime juice.
Salt to taste.

Grind all the above ingredients to a paste.

Moong Dal Chutney

1 cup sprouted moong.
2 red and 2 green chilies.
2 tblsps. grated coconut.
1 tblsp. tamrind pulp.
Salt to taste.

Grind the above ingredients to a paste.

Chapter 8

SALADS

Wheat Sprout Salad

1 cup wheat sprout.

2 carrots, grated.

2 tblsps. roasted til.

Handful of coriander leaves, chopped.

1 tblsp. each of honey and raisin.

Mix all the above ingredients and decorate with raisin and til.

Crunchy Salad

2 cups wheat sprouts.

1 cup mung sprouts.

1 capsicum, shreded.

Handful of chopped coriander leaves.

2 green onions, shreded.

Lime juice to suit the taste.

1 medium tomato, chopped.

Mix together all the above ingredients.

Mung Sprouts and Coconut Salad

1 cup mung sprouts.

¼ cup grated coconut.

½ cup finely shredded cabbage.

3 green onions, finely sliced.

Handful of chopped coriander leaves.

1 tsp. grated ginger.

1 green chili, minced.

Lime juice to taste.

Mix together all the above ingredients.

Alfa Alfa Salad

3 cups alfa alfa sprouts.

1 cucumber, chopped.

1 cup chopped lettuce.

1 capsicum, shredded.

1 tomato, chopped.

2 green onions, chopped.

½ cup chopped cabbage.

Lime juice and salt to taste.

Mix together all the above ingredients.

Alfa Alfa and Peas Salad

1 cup each of alfa alfa sprouts, shredded cabbage and lettuce.

1 cup peas.

2 tomatoes, chopped.

2 cucumbers, chopped.

Salt and lime juice to taste.

Mix together all the above ingredients.

Winters Delight

1 lettuce cut in pieces.

1 cup cauliflower flowerets.

2 carrots cut into strips.

6 tomatoes, chopped.

1 cup alfa alfa sprouts.

6 red reddishes, sliced.

1 capsicum, shredded.

1 cup sweat corn.

Salt and lime juice to taste.

Mix together all the above ingredients.

Salad Badshahi

Chop lettuce, spinach and reddish leaves and place in an oval serving dish. In the center of the plate put Russian Salad, arrange tomato slices around the salad. Top these with paper thin slices of one each of beetroot, cucumber and onion. Decorate the whole with chopped tomato.

Stuffed Capsicum Salad

2 medium capsicums.

2 tomatoes.

1 tblsp. oil.

Juice of ½ lime.

Pinch of ajinomotto.

Salt to taste.

For filling take:

150 grams cream cheese,

1 small onion, minced.

1 small cucumber, minced.

1 tender beetroot, minced.

Handful of minced coriander leaves.

1 green chili, minced.

Salt to taste.

Mix cream cheese with all the filling ingredients. Slice the capsicums into halves and scoop out the seeds. Cut into neat strips. Apply the cheese thickly on each strip. Cut the tomato into wedges and mix with oil, lime juice, salt and ajinomotto. Serve the capsicums surrounded by tomatoes.

Stuffed Tomato Salad

Take small, firm tomatoes. Cut off a thin slice from the top of each tomato. Remove seeds and pulp and put a little salt in each tomato shell. Allow them to stand upside down for about 15 minutes. Fill with Russian salad and serve on a bed of lettuce leaves.

Tomato and Pineapple Salad

Put some lettuce in a salad bowl. Cut the tomatoes into quarter without cutting through. Fill the centers with Russian salad and decorate with chopped pineapple.

Orange and Apple Salad

1 cup orange meat.

1 cup sliced apples.

1 cup seedless grapes.

½ cup chopped walnuts.

1 cup mayonnaise sauce.

4 tblsps. cream.

Salt and pepper to taste.

Mix together all the above ingredients and serve cold.

Banana and Apple Salad

1 cup chopped apples.

1 cup mayonnaise sauce.

½ cup chopped calary.

½ cup chopped walnuts.

2 bananas, diced.

2 tblsps. cream.

Salt and papper to taste.

Mix together all the above ingredients and serve cold.

Chapter 9

RAITAS

Banana Raita

2 medium bananas, peeled and sliced.

2 cups curd.

2 green chilies, minced.

½ inch finely sliced ginger.

2 tblsps. powdered mint.

1 tsp. roasted and ground cumin seeds.

Salt and chili powder to taste.

1 tsp. sugar.

Beat curd with 2 tblsps. water and seasonings and sugar till smooth. Stir in the rest of the ingredients with the exception of cumin seeds. Sprinkle roasted cumin seeds on top before serving.

Sweet Curd

1 cup thick curd. A few drops of essence of saffron.

15 grams each of sliced almonds, pistachios, charoli and cashew nuts.

1 tblsp. raisins.

Sugar to suit the taste.

Put curds in a clean piece of cloth and tie loosely. Hang the bag for a couple of hours in order to enable all the liquid to drip through. Beat up the curds with the help of a fork and mix in the rest of the ingredients. Serve chilled.

Fruit Raita

2 cup thick curd.

1 tblsp. honey and a few drops of either essence of rose, kewda or saffron.

1 small plantain, peeled and diced.

1 ripe mangoe, peeled and diced.

2 rings/canned pineapple, diced.

Mix together curd, cream, honey and essence and beat till smooth. Put in the fruits. Mix nicely and serve chilled. This is a delicious raita which is excellent for health and beauty.

Dilpasand Raita

2 cup thick curd.

1 tblsp. honey.

2 tblsps. each of finely sliced almonds, pistachios and charoli.

2 tblsps. golden raisins.

4 slices of canned pineapple, diced.

2 bananas, peeled and diced.

12 sliced strawberries.

A couple of whole strawberries rolled in little brown sugar.

Mix together curd, honey, nuts and raisins. Put alternate layers of strawberries, pineapple and bananas in shiny dessert glasses. Alternate each layer of fruit with a layer of chilled curd. Decorate the top with a strawberry rolled in brown sugar and see your guests raving.

Onion Raita

2 cups curd.

2 medium onion, minced.

Handful of coriander leaves.

A few mint leaves.

2 green chilies, minced.

½-inch piece ginger, sliced.

1 tsp. ground and roasted cumin seeds.

½ tsp. ground mustard seeds.

Salt and chili powder to taste.

Soak onions in water for 5 minutes. Squeeze out the water and mix with the remaining ingredients; serve cold.

Raita Dilwala

2 cups curd. 1 red tomato, cubed.

1 small onion, minced.

2 green chilies, minced.

1 small cucumber.

Handful of coriander leaves.

A few mint leaves.

1 tsp. roasted and grounded cumin seeds.

½ tsp. dry ginger powder.

Dash of pepper powder.

Salt and chili powder to taste.

Mix all the above ingredients together and decorate with green leaves.

Pudina Raita

1 cup curds.

30 mint leaves.

4 green chilies.

Salt to taste.

Grind mint and chilies together, mix into the curd along with salt.

Banana Raita

2 medium ripe bananas, peeled and sliced.

2 cups curd. 2 green chilies, minced.

½ tsp. grated ginger.

2 tblsps. powdered mint.

1 tsp. roasted and grounded cumin seeds.

1 tsp. castor sugar.

Salt and chili powder to taste.

Mix together all the above ingredients and sprinkle on top roasted cumin seeds.

Pudina and Raisin Raita

1 cup mint leaves.

2 cup curd. 25 grams raisins.

1 tsp. cumin seeds.

Salt and chili powder to taste.

Grind raisin, mint and cumin seeds. Mix into the curds along with the remaining ingredients. Serve cold.

Khajur Raita

280 grams curd. 75 grams stoned dates.

¼ coconut.

Salt to taste.

Grind dates and coconut to a very fine paste. Mix into the curd along with salt. Serve chilled.

Redish Raita

1 cup curd. 1 tender radish, scraped and grated finely.

2 green chilies, minced.

Handful of minced coriander leaves.

Salt to taste.

Mix all the above ingredients together.

Mango Raita

Mango/jackfruit or pineapple Raita.

1 cup curd. 1 big ripe mango, diced, 1 tsp. roasted and grounded cumin seeds.

1 tblsp. castor sugar.

Salt to taste.

Mix all the above ingredients together.

Tomato Raita

1 cup curd. 1 big tomato, sliced ½ tsp.
chili paste.

1 tsp. grounded mustard seeds.

A few coriander leaves.

Salt to taste.

Mix together all the above ingredients.

Carrot and Groundnut Raita

150 grams finely grated carrots.

2 cups curd. 25 grams powdered roasted groundnuts.

2 green chilies, minced.

1 tsp. castor sugar.

1 tsp. powdered cumin seeds.

Handful of finely sliced coriander leaves.

Mix together all the above ingredients and serve cold.

Cucumber and Coconut Raita

100 grams grated cucumber.

2 cups curd. 1 medium tomato, cubed.

1 tsp. grated ginger.

Handful of coriander leaves.

1 tblsp. grated coconut.

1 tsp. castor sugar.

Salt to taste.

Mix together all the above ingredients and serve cold.

Cabbage and Nut Raita

1 cup finely shredded cabbage.

2 cups curd. 1 tblsp.

chopped cashewnuts.

1 tblsp. chopped groundnuts.

1 tblsp. chopped raisins.

2 green chillies.

½ inch piece ginger.

Hanful of coriander leaves.

1 tsp. cumin seeds.

Salt to taste.

Grind together chilies, coriander and ginger with cumin seeds. Mix with all the above ingredients and serve cold.

Ginger Raita

1 cup grated coconut.

2 cups curd.

2 tblsps. ground ginger.

25 grams raisins.

Handful of coriander leaves.

Salt and chili powder to taste.

Mix all the above ingredients and serve cold.

Tomato and Coconut Raita

2 cups curd. 2 tblsps.

grated coconut.

1 medium tomato, cubed.

2 green chilies, minced.

2 green onions, sliced, salt, pepper and chili powder to taste.

Mix all the ingredients together and serve cold.

Cucumber and Carrot Raita

2 cups curd.

1 cucumber, grated.

1 carrot, grated.

A few springs coriander leaves.

1 tsp. ground cumin seeds.

2 green chilies, minced.

Salt to taste.

Mix all the above ingredients and serve cold.

Cucumber and Tomato Raita

100 grams grated cucumber.

100 grams curds.

Handful of sliced coriander leaves.

½ inch piece ginger, minced.

1 firm tomato, diced.

1 tblsp. grated coconut.

1 tsp. sugar.

Salt to taste.

Mix all the above ingredients together.

Capsicum Raita

2 Capsicum, cut into strips, 100 grams curd.

½ tsp. garam masala.

Handful coriander leaves.

1 tsp. sugar.

1 tsp. roasted and ground cumin seeds.

Salt and chili powder to taste.

Mix all the above ingredients together.

Coconut and Dal Raita

½ coconut, grated.

50 grams urad dal, soaked in water for 5 to 6 hours.

½ cup coriander leaves.

4 green chilies.

½ inch piece ginger.

1 tsp. cumin seeds.

1 cup curd.

8 curry leaves.

½ tsp. mustard seeds.

1 tsp. coriander seeds.

2 red chilies.

Salt to taste.

Drain out the water from the dal and grind all the above ingredients to a paste with the exception of curd. Mix into the curd and serve chilled.

Chapter 10

CHICKEN RECIPES

Roast Chicken

1 small chicken with skin removed
250 grams mixed vegetables like carrots, French beans, cabbage and peas
1 big tomato
1 tablespoon grated ginger
1 medium onion, minced
2 green chilies, minced
½ teaspoon each of garam masala and turmeric powder
Handful of coriander leaves
Salt and chili powder to taste
2 teaspoons butter

Heat 1 teaspoon butter and fry the onion and ginger till soft. Add tomato along with the rest of the spices and cook till dry. Add vegetables and ¼ cup water. Cook till tender and dry. Clean the chicken nicely and rub both inside out with salt and pepper. Put in the stuffing, tie up, rub the outside with remaining butter and bake in a hot oven till fork tender.

Murg Tikka Kabab

1 small chicken, boned and cubed

8 baby onions

½ teaspoon garlic juice

½ teaspoon ginger juice

1 seeded capsicum cut into pieces

½ teaspoon each of grounded cumin and coriander seeds

1 tablespoon soya sauce

1 teaspoon oil

Salt and chili powder to taste

Mix ginger with spices, ginger and garlic juice and soya sauce. Set aside for 4 hours. Place the chicken pieces on skewers alternating the chicken pieces with onions and capsicums. Brush with oil and grill on open fire or in an oven till the chicken is brown and tender.

Sweet and Sour Chicken

2 cups chopped vegetables like capsicums, carrots, French beans and cabbage.

1 cup diced cooked chicken

For sauce take :

¼ cup vinegar

¼ cup tomato sauce

1 tablespoon sugar

¼ teaspoon prepared mustard

1 teaspoon corn flour dissolved in ½ cup water

Salt and chili powder to taste

Heat 1 teaspoon oil, add the vegetables, mix well and steam till cooked. Mix in the chicken then prepare the sauce. Mix all the sauce ingredients, cook till thick and then mix in the vegetables and chicken. Serve hot.

Tandoori Chicken

1 medium chicken

2 tablespoons lime juice

1 teaspoon garam masala

1 teaspoon grounded green chilies

1 teaspoon grounded methi leaves

1 teaspoon cardamom powder

½ teaspoon red food colouring

1 teaspoon grounded saffron

2 cups curd

Salt and chili powder to taste

Skin chicken and remove all fats. Clean the insides. Make deep gashes or slits on the chicken and rub with lime juice, salt and chili powder. Mix together the remaining ingredients and let the chicken marinate in it for 45 minutes. Bake for 1 hour in 350^0 F oven. Half way through the baking rub 1 teaspoon butter on the chicken. When it is cooked dust with chaat masala and serve with green chutney and a mixed salad of raw onion slices, cucumber, tomato and lime.

Crunchy Baked Chicken

1 small chicken with skin removed

Cornflour

Milk with cream removed

Potato wafers

1 teaspoon garam masala

1 teaspoon dhania-jeera powder

2 tablespoons lime juice

Salt and chili powder to taste

Make slits on the chicken. Rub on it lime juice mixed with all the spices and salt. Set aside for 2 hours. Roll in cornflour. Crush the wafers with a rolling pin on a sheet of grease paper. Dip the chicken in milk, then coat thickly and evenly with wafer crumbs. Bake in a moderate oven till tender.

Dahi Murg

1 small chicken, with skin removed and cut into serving portions

2 big tomatoes

1 cup curd made with milk with cream removed

1 medium onion

4 flakes garlic

¾ cm piece ginger

4 green chilies

Handful of coriander leaves

1 teaspoon dhania-jeera powder

½ teaspoon garam masala

Salt and chili powder to taste

Grind onion, ginger and garlic. Mix all the above ingredients together and cook till the chicken is tender. Heat 1 teaspoon oil and put over the chicken. Serve hot.

Chapter 11

FISH RECIPES

Fish Curry

2 slices pomfret.

100 grams mixed vegetables.

½ tsp. grated ginger.

1 crushed garlic flake.

1 tblsp. curd.

1 small tomato.

1 small minced onion.

¼ tsp. turmeric powder.

A few coriander leaves. Pinch of garam masala.

Salt and pepper to taste.

Apply salt and turmeric on the fish and set aside for 15 minutes. Heat 1 tsp. oil and fry ginger, garlic and onions. Add tomato and curds and cook till dry. Put in the vegetables. Mix well and pour in ½ cup water. When both vegetables and fish are done, sprinkle on top coriander leaves and garam masala.

Boiled Fish

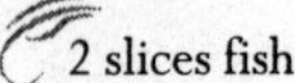

2 slices fish.

1 small carrot, halved.

A pinch of nutmeg.

A few peppercorns.

Salt and lime juice to taste.

Put fish in 1 cup water along with spices, salt, carrots and onions and boil in water till soft and dry. Discard vegetables and peppercorns. If you like you can put tomato ketchup on the fish.

Baked Fish

2 slices pomfret.

2 tblsps. milk.

1 tsp. butter.

Bread crumbs.

Salt and pepper to taste.

Rub salt on the fish. Dip in milk roll lightly in crumbs and put in a greased baking dish. Dot with butter and bake in a very hot oven on both the sides till brown and crisp.

Chutney Fish

2 slices pomfret.

¼ cup coriander leaves.

1 green chili. ¼ tsp.

cumin seeds.

1 flake garlic.

¼ inch ginger.

piece. A few mint leaves.

1 small onion.

A big pinch chili powder.

Salt and lime juice to taste.

Grind all the ingredients with the exception of fish to a paste. Apply the paste to both the sides of the fish. Put both the slices separately in a well-greased brown paper. Tie up and steam for 10 minutes on either side.

Garlic Fish

2 slices pomfret.

6 flakes grated garlic.

1 small tomato, minced.

Handful of chopped coriander leaves.

A pinch chili powder.

1 tsp. turmeric powder.

Salt to taste.

Heat 1 tsp. oil and fry the garlic, add the rest of the ingredients with the exception of fish; when the mixture turns dry add fish and add ½ cup water. Cook till tender. Serve hot.

Mustard Fish

2 slices pomfret.

1 tsp. mustard seeds.

6 flakes garlic.

1 small tomato grated.

Handful of coriander leaves.

¼ tsp. turmeric powder.

A big pinch chili powder.

Salt to taste.

Heat 1 tsp. oil and garlic, fry then add tomato, salt and spices. Cook till dry, add fish and add 1 cup water. Cook till soft. Fry mustard in ½ tsp. oil and put over the fish.

Tomato Fish

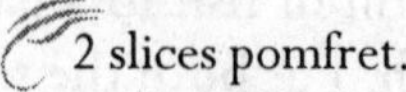

2 slices pomfret.

50 grams tomatoes, chopped.

¼ tsp. each of grated ginger and garlic.

Handful of chopped coriander leaves.

¼ tsp. turmeric powder.

A big pinch chili powder.

Salt to taste.

Heat 1 tsp. oil and fry ginger, garlic and chilies till soft; add all the spices, salt and fish; fry lightly and then put tomatoes on top. Cover and cook over a slow fire till the tomatoes are soft and the fish is cooked.

Chapter 11

MUTTON RECIPES

Mutton with Vegetables

250 grams lean mutton.

100 grams mixed vegetables of your choice.

¼ coconut.

A few mint leaves.

A few curry leaves.

¼ tsp. turmeric powder.

1 small onion.

Salt and pepper to taste.

A pinch of garam masala.

Grind coconut and extract juice. Set this thick juice aside put 1 cup hot water on squeezed out coconut scrapings and set aside for a few minutes. Then squeeze out the milk. This is known as thin milk. Put mutton, salt and spices in this thin milk and cook till almost tender. Put in the vegetables and mint leaves and continue cooking till both mutton and vegetables are done. Fry onions and curry leaves in half a teaspoon of oil to a light brown colour, put over the mutton and serve at once.

Mutton Cake

1 cup minced lean mutton.

1 slice bread.

1 small tomato.

½ tsp. grated 1 minced green chili.

A few coriander leaves.

Salt and pepper to taste.

Soak bread in milk and squeeze dry, mix into the mince along with the rest of the above ingredients. Put in a greased mould and put the mould in a tray of hot water and bake in an oven till set.

Irish Stew

250 grams lean mutton.

250 grams mixed vegetables of your choice.

Salt and pepper to taste.

Put a layer of mutton and vegetables in a heavy saucepan till all the ingredients are used up. Cover with hot water and cook till both the vegetables and mutton are cooked.

Sheekh Kababs

250 grams minced lean mutton.

1 tblsp. ground onions.

1 green chili, minced.

1 tsp. ginger minced.

Handful of sliced coriander leaves.

1 tblsp. thick curd.

1 tblsp. roasted gramflour.

Pinch of pepper powder.

Pinch of garam masala.

Salt to taste.

Mix together all the above ingredients with 1 tsp. oil. With wet hands mould the meat mixture around greased skewers pressing and shaping to the size of sheikh kababs. Grill over open flame turning frequently till they turn golden, serve hot.

Mutton Hamburgers

250 grams lean mutton, minced.

1 slice bread, soaked in water and squeezed dry.

2 flakes garlic, minced.

½ tsp. minced ginger 1 small onion, minced.

1 tblsp. ketchup.

Handful of sliced coriander leaves.

1 tsp oil.

Salt and pepper to taste.

Mix together all the above ingredients with the exception of oil. Shape into round flat cutlets and keep aside 20 minutes. Put in a moderate oven after greasing the top side lightly with oil, when the top turns golden, turn over and grease the other side also; remove from the oven when both the sides are well browned.

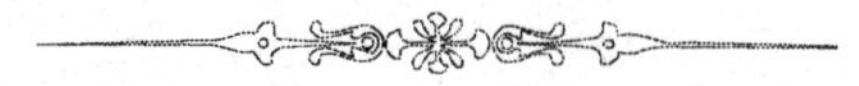

Chapter 12

INDIAN BREADS

Puffed Rotli

250 grams flour.
Rice flour.
Melted ghee.
Salt to taste.

Mix salt with flour, rub in 1 tblsp. ghee and add enough water to form a stiff dough. Divide the dough into small balls and roll out each ball into a small round. Apply melted ghee on one side of the round and sprinkle a little rice flour over it. Cover with another round and then roll out as thinly as you can with the help of a little dry flour, but roll out from the sides and not from the middle. Put the rotli on a dry girdle, when the undersize starts turning brown, turn over and press oil over with a clean cloth till it is nicely baked and pufled. Remove from the girdle and serve hot. This rotli is usually eaten with aamb rus. To make the rus, roast sweet mangoes on a hot girdle till they turn soft and pulpy. Squeeze out the juice and strain through a cloth. In each cup or juice mix in a little grounded dry ginger and salt to taste.

Khakre

1 cup flour.

1 small bunch cleaned and sliced methi or fenugreek leaves.

2 green chilies, minced.

A handful of sliced coriander leaves.

Tsp. each of dhania jeera powder and turmeric powder.

Salt, lime juice and sugar to taste.

Mix together all the above ingredients and then add enough water to form a stiff dough. Divice the cough into small balls and roll out each ball into a round chapatti. Bake each chapatti lightly on both the sides. Apply ghee liberally to each side of the chapatti and stack chapaties one over the other and set aside for a few hours. Then re-roast the chapaties over the girdle with the help of a clean cloth till crisp and biscuit coloured. Remove cool and store in airtight tin. They last for 1 week.

Bajre ki Roti with Garlic Chutney

For roti take :

2 cups *bajra* flour

Pinch of salt

For chutney take :

12 flakes garlic

6 green chilies

Handful of coriander leaves

Strained juice of ½ lime

Grind all the *chutney* ingredients together. Mix flour and salt. Add enough water to form a stiff dough. Divide into balls. Dip the balls in wheat flour and roll out into a thick roti. Bake on both the sides. Smear with very little butter and serve with *chutney*.

Sweet Joyar Roti

2 cups *jowar* flour

6 tablespoons grated jaggery

Dash of salt

1 teaspoon cumin seeds

Soak jaggery with 1 cup water. When it dissolves, strain and set aside. Mix salt and cumin seeds with flour. Add enough jaggery to form a stiff dough. Divide into big balls. Dip in wheat flour and roll out into thick *roti*. Bake on both the sides on a hot tava. Smear with ¼ teaspoon butter and serve with curds and sour pickle.

Chapati

250 granrs flour

Add enough water into the flour to form a stiff dough. Divide the flour into small balls, dip in dry flour and roll out into a thin round *roti*. Bake on a hot tava on both the sides till slightly brown, then put the *chapati* on an open flame till it puffs up like a balloon. Serve hot with vegetable or meat dish. If you want to preserve them for a few days, then smear each *chapati* lightly with oil after it is baked and stack one on top of the other. Wrap in polythene bag and store in the fridge, when you want to use them just heat them over the tava and serve.

Makki ki Roti

250 grams maize or *makai* flour

Salt to taste

Mix together salt and flour; add enough water to form a stiff dough. Divide into small balls. Roll in wheat flour and then roll out into a thick round *roti* being careful not to break it. Bake on both the sides on a hot tava till both the sides are well-cooked. Smear ¼ teaspoon butter on each *roti* and serve with sarsoan-ka-sag. See section on vegetarian dishes for sarsoan-ka-sag.

Masala Jowar Roti

2 cups *jowar* flour

Small onion, minced

2 green chillies, minced

Handful of coriander leaves, minced

1 bunch fresh green garlic, minced

Salt to taste

Mix together all the above ingredients with enough water to form a stiff dough. Divide into big balls. Roll in wheat flour and roll out into thick *roti* being careful not to break it. Bake it on both the sides on a hot tava till well-cooked. Smear top with ¼ teaspoon butter and serve with *raita* of choice (see the section on Raita in "Curd based recipies")

Masala Roti

1 cup flour

1 tablespoon oil

½ cup very finely sliced *methi* leaves

1 green chilli, minced

1 teaspoon minced onions

Salt and chilli powder to taste

Mix together all the above ingredients with enough water to form a stiff dough. Divide the dough into small balls and roll out each ball into a thin *chapati*. Heat tava and bake the *chapati* on both the sides very sparingly. Make all the *chapaties* in the same manner and pile on a plate. Now re-roast all the chapaties till brown on both the sides. Serve with *raita* of your choice.

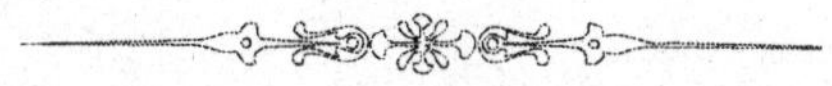

Chapter 12

RICE RECIPES

Khichadi

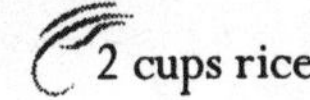

2 cups rice

½ cup either moong dal, masur dal, toohar or arhar dal

1 teaspoon ghee

¼ teaspoon cumin seeds

½ teaspoon turmeric powder

1 small onion, sliced

Salt to taste

Wash and soak rice and dal separately for a few hours. Drain and put in a vessel along with salt and turmeric powder. Add enough water to stand 1-inch above the level of the rice. Allow it to boil, reduce heat and cook till tender and dry. Fry onion and cumin seeds in ghee and put over the *Khichadi*. Serve with curd.

Paella

1 cup boiled rice

1 cup mixed vegetables like peas, carrots, French beans and cauliflower

¼ cup cooked chicken

1 cup cooked prawns

1 hard-boiled egg

A big pinch saffron

1 medium tomato

1 small onion, minced

¼ inch piece ginger, minced

2 teaspoons oil

Salt and pepper to taste

Heat oil and fry ginger and onion till soft. Add tomato and cook till soft. Mix in the vegetables and salt. Add very little water and cook till done. Mix in the rice, chicken and prawn, pepper and saffron. Decorate with egg.

Potato Pullao

1 cup boiled rice

1 medium potato, boiled, peeled and cubed

Handful of coriander leaves

2 green chillies, minced

1 tiny onion, minced

¼ teaspoon minced ginger

¼ teaspoon cumin seeds

2 teaspoons oil

1 tablespoon *dhania-jeera* powder

1 teaspoon *garam masala*

Salt and chilli powder to taste

Heat oil; add cumin seeds; when the seeds stop popping add onion and ginger and chillies, cook till soft. Add potatoes with spices and coriander leaves. Cook for 2 to 3 minutes, mix in the rice nicely and heat thoroughly.

Fish Pullao American

2 cups boiled rice

250 grains fish fillets, cut into narrow ribbons

250 grams mixed vegetables like peas, carrots and capsicums

¼ teaspoon saffron strands dissolved in 1 teaspoon hot water

1 small onion

4 flakes garlic

4 green chillies

Handful of coriander leaves

100 grams tomatoes

1 teaspoon butter

Salt to taste

Grind onion, garlic and chillies. Heat butter and fry the grounded paste till soft. Add tomatoes and cook till thick. Put in the salt and coriander leaves. Set the fish inside along with ¼ cup water and cook till the fish is done. Now steam cook the vegetables and mix them into the rice along with saffron. Put the fish in the centre of a serving plate and arrange a border of rice around it.

Curd Rice

1-½ cup boiled rice

1 cup curd made with milk with the cream removed

2 green chillies, minced

Handful of coriander leaves

1 small cucumber, peeled and sliced

¼ teaspoon mustard seeds

1 sprig curry leaves

Salt to taste

Mix together rice, curd, chillies, coriander and cucumber. Heat 1 teaspoon oil and fry the mustard seeds and curry leaves. Put over the rice and serve cold.

Chicken aod Vegetable Pullao

1 cup boiled rice

½ cup cooked lean chicken, shredded

250 grams mixed vegetables like carrots, capsicums and peas

1 big tomato, sliced

1 hard-boiled egg, sliced

¼ teaspoon saffron strands dissolved in little hot water

1 teaspoon dhania jeera powder

½ teaspoon garam masala

Salt and chilli powder to taste

1 teaspoon butter

Heat butter, add tomato and cook till soft. Add the vegetables and spices. Mix well and sprinkle a little water on top. Cook till crisp-tender. Mix in the rice, saffron and chicken. Heat thoroughly and decorate with boiled egg.

Creole Rice

1 cup boiled rice

¼ cup cooked mushrooms

¼ cup shredded capsicums

1 sprig celery

2 green onions, sliced thinly

1 egg, hardboiled and quartered

For sauce take:

1 teaspoon butter

1 teaspoon flour

½ cup pureed or pulped tomatoes

½ teaspoon prepared mustard

½ teaspoon Worcestershire Or vegetable sauce

Salt and chilli powder to taste

Heat 1 teaspoon butter and add onions, cook till soft. Add capsicums and celery and salt. Sprinkle a little water on top and cook till crisp tender. Mix in the rice and mushrooms. Heat thoroughly. Now prepare the sauce. Heat 1 teaspoon butter and add flour. Fry lightly and then add the remaining sauce ingredients and cook till thick. Put the sauce over the rice and decorate with eggs.

Chapter 13

SWEETS

Nutty Curd

2 cups curd. 4 tblsps.
honey. 2 apples, grated.
1 tblsp. lime juice.
2 tblsps. roasted sunflower seeds.

Beat the curd with honey. Mix together apple, lime juice and mix into the curd. Decorate with seeds.

Fruit and Honey Delight

2 cups curd.
1 tblsp. brandy.
4 tblsps. honey.
250 grams seedlass grapes.
A few roasted almonds.

Mix together all the above ingredients with the exception of almonds. Put in small individual dishes and decorate with almonds. Serve chilled.

Honey Kheer

½ liter skimmed milk.

2 tblsps. grounded rice.

3 tblsps. roasted and grounded til.

2 tblsps. grounded almonds.

2 tblsps. melon seeds.

6 tblsps. honey.

Put milk with sugar to boil, reduce heat and add the remaining ingredients. Cook till thick. Serve decorated with rose petals.

Honey Lassi

2 cups curd.

3 tblsps. honey.

2 tblsps. each of melon seeds and til.

1 glass water.

Mix together in the blender. Add a few drops essence of rose. Serve chilled.

Honey Lemonade

Juice of 1 lime.

4 tblsps. honey.

Carbonated drink like soda.

Whisk the above ingredients in the blender and blend till smooth.

Honey Coffee

1 glass cold milk.

¼ cup prepared coffee.

4 tblsps. honey.

Whisk in the blender till smooth. Serve chilled.

Honey and Tomato Shake

1 cup cold milk.

4 tblsps. tomato juice.

1 tsp. lime juice.

2 tsps. honey.

Whisk all the above ingredients in the blender.

Fruit and Honey Shake

2 cups curds.

1 cup skimmed milk.

½ cup fruit juice of your choice.

4 tblsps. honey.

Pinch of ginger.

Whisk all the above ingredients in the blender till smooth. Sprinkle ginger powder on top before serving.

Honey Fruit Punch

1 cup honey.

1 cup pineapple juice.

2 cups sweet lime juice.

1 cup orange juice.

1 cup grape juice.

3 tblsps. lime juice.

25 grams each of powdered cashew nuts and almonds.

1 cup finely sliced fruits of your choice.

Mix together all the above ingredients. Chill before serving.

Til Chikki

½ cup honey.

1 cup grated jaggery.

¾ cup roasted til.

2 tblsps. each of sliced almonds, pistachios and raisins.

Mix together jaggery with 2 tblsps. water and dissolve on a slow fire. Add honey and cardamom seeds, when it is dissolved mix in the remaining ingredients. Pour on a greased sheet and flatten it out on a thin sheet. When cold, break into pieces.

Honey Ice Cream

½ liter milk.

½ cup each of finely chopped dates and figs.

1 cup honey.

25 grams each of finely sliced almonds and pistachios.

Boil milk till thick, mix in the remaining ingredients and freeze in the freezer tray, when almost frozen, beat with a fork to a smooth paste, cover with silver foil and refreeze till firm.

HEALTH HARMONY

Health Harmony is an imprint of **B. Jain Publishers (P) Ltd.,** which is a 35-year-old publishing house. Our books are very popular for two reasons. Firstly, the prices are very reasonable and secondly, the quality of material and content is excellent.

Tree in the **Health Harmony** signifies Holistic life and that is what the mankind should aim at. This tree is lush green which signifies total health. Also, its roots are well fixed to the ground which motivates us to be down to earth and respect our roots. Thirdly, this tree is in harmony with its atmosphere i.e. air, water, soil. This helps us to understand that we have to preserve our environment if we have to remain healthy and in harmony.

Our publishing house conceived the idea of Health Harmony two years back to provide interesting and top-quality reading material for seekers and believers of health and holistic living.

Under the banner of **Health Harmony**, we have expanded our collection to encompass Health, Sprituality, Astrology, Feng Shui, Vastu, Palmistry, Numerology, Management, Career & Travel related books. Till now, we have added more than 400 books to our **Helath Harmony** collection. We were the first to publish books on Reiki, Tai Chi, Acupressure and books by Rudolf Steiner who is a great European Philospher.

It is our endevour to provide to the masses of Indian Subcontinent (India, Pakistan, Bangladesh, Nepal, Bhutan, Sri Lanka, etc.) the best published works of the world at low price without compromising with the quality of the books.

One of the main reason for the popularity of **Health Harmony** books with the readers is that these are written by authors who are authority on the published subject. Like some others publications, we do not encourage compilation and cut-paste work.

For Free Catalogue details refer overleaf

www.bjainbooks.com

FREE CATALOGUE COUPON

Yes, I am interested in Health Harmony titles. Please rush me the catalogue.

FREE CATALOGUE ORDER FORM

(Write in Capitals)

Name ....

Complete Mailing Address ....

....

....

....

....

.... Pin ....

Ph. (Res.) .... Ph. (Off.) ....

E-mail. ....

Date .... Signature

Mail this coupan to

HEALTH HARMONY

an Imprint of

B. JAIN PUBLISHERS (P) LTD.
1921, Chuna Mandi, St. 10th Paharganj, New Delhi-110 055
Ph.: 3670572, 3670430, 3683200, 3683300
Fax: 011-3610471 & 3683400
Website: www.bjainbooks. com, Email:bjain@vsnl.com